# A Guide to Profitable
# Self Employment

*And How to Achieve the*
*Self Confidence to Create*
*Abundance & Prosperity Regardless*
*Of Your Present Circumstances!*

**Martin Woodward**

ISBN: 978-1-291-64006-9

# Contents

# Introduction

Becoming self employed certainly has advantages over being employed, but I've no doubt it's not for everyone. Some of the main advantages are:

- You'll never be made redundant again;
- You don't have to bow and grovel to any hierarchy;
- You'll never have to write another CV (I've never needed one ever), or suffer the humiliation of interviews and rejections;
- There are certain tax advantages;
- Working hard becomes more enjoyable as you know that *you* will reap the rewards;
- You could become financially independent.

But it's equally important that you are aware of the disadvantages, some of which are:

- It can take some time to become established;
- You may have to work long hours initially for very low returns;
- Generating business may be harder than you think;
- You will not be paid for holidays, and when you do have one, you'll probably have to make arrangements for someone to deal with your business enquiries etc.;
- As well as operating your business, you will also have to spend time keeping your accounts in good order and have to calculate PAYE and VAT if you employ anyone;
- You will have to take care of your own pension arrangements;
- You will have to build a reputation for quality, reliability and fair prices in order to survive;
- You may not survive - it's harder than you think in fact 2/3rds of new businesses fail in the first year.

Looking at the above, it seems that there are more disadvantages than advantages, but having said all this, for me the pros outweigh the cons and I wouldn't have it any other way.

If you have few or no qualifications, you either have to spend a lifetime in menial employment - if you're lucky - or become self employed and create your own success!

Every business involves a certain risk element. But the valuable information given herein will help you ensure that any risk is 'calculated' and not pure 'speculation'.

Furthermore the contents that follow have been written with a lifetime of experience by someone who has not only *survived*, but *prospered* during several recessions in a number of different occupations, mainly requiring no qualifications.

Also included are several **free bonus** items including:

- 6 x 30 minute powerful mp3 recordings guaranteed unavailable elsewhere;

- Links to 5 of the most powerful inspirational books ever written.

In fact if you read and absorb all of this information, you would find it more difficult to fail than succeed, regardless of your current financial or educational circumstances.

# Choosing your Business

You may well have already considered what type of business you would like to operate, but here's a few points that may help you choose, or change your mind:

- Can it be run from home? (spare room, garage or garden office), if so you will have a much greater chance of success;

- If you do need business premises, check suitability and location for your chosen business and look into rent, rates and planning consent;

- Will the business generate repeat trade? - if so how often e.g. - you can sell *bread* to the same customer every day, but they will only need their *hair cutting* once every 6 weeks whereas a *car* will probably last them 3 years or longer!;

- Will your business be seasonal - and if so to what extent? Perhaps consider two complimentary occupations - sell ice cream in the summer and hot chestnuts in the winter;

- Will you need a license or training or qualifications? There are many businesses where you need none of these;

- Will you need machinery and will it be messy etc.? I've run sign businesses from spare bedrooms and a printing business from a garage. Every now and then the wife threw a fit, but beyond that it was workable;

- Will it be profitable? - See further chapters about profits;

- Is it an up and coming profession/occupation or on its way out? i.e., milk deliveries and Post Offices are dying a death whereas chimney sweeps are enjoying a rebirth;

- Can you drop it and pick it up again without re-building a customer base? If this is what you want, a metered taxi (hackney carriage) is an excellent option, you just get in and go;

- Is there much competition? This is nothing to be afraid of, just offer a good, reliable service at a fair price - you don't necessarily have to be the cheapest;

- Will it bring in an immediate income or will it take a long time to build a client base?
- Will you have enough finances?
- Will your clientele be local, national or worldwide?

Thoroughly research your chosen business and make sure that you would be doing it for the right reasons. If I was a multimillionaire, I would still be doing what I am doing now, because this is what I want to do, and this is of course the best reason. There's an old Chinese proverb: 'If a man enjoys his occupation, he will never have to work a day in his life!' - It's true!

I'm 64 years old and have been a self employed sole trader all my life except for just over a year after I first left school when I briefly worked in the Post Office and a music publishers.

The Occupations I've been involved in over the last 44 years are:
- Professional musician (UK and Europe);
- Taxi Driver (hackney carriage South London);
- Café owner;
- Driving School proprietor (12 cars, 30 years);
- Sign Making/Printing (UK & Cyprus);
- Property landlord (several properties UK & Europe);
- Stock market (dabbled);
- Self Publisher of relaxation recordings, business guides and music books (via websites).

Some of these were operated concurrently.

You may notice that most of the above are mainly 'service' based rather than 'sale' based businesses. Basically, whatever business you decide to go for, it will fall into one of the following categories:
- Service Based;
- Part Service, part Sales;
- Sales Based;
- Production/manufacturing;
- Unearned income.

Following are a few examples of occupations in these categories:

**Service Based Businesses**

- Accountant;
- Baby sitter;*
- Beautician/nail artist;*
- Book keeper;*
- Builder;
- Carer;
- Carpenter;*
- Carpet cleaner;*
- Chimney sweep;*
- Cleaner;*
- Computer repairs/tuition;*
- Dog groomer (mobile);*
- Dog kennels;
- Driving instructor;
- Dry cleaners;*
- Entertainment agent/organizer;*
- Financial consultant;
- Gardener;*
- Hairdresser (mobile);
- Holistic therapist;*
- House/dog sitter;*
- Hypnotist;*
- Introduction agency;*
- Ironing service;*
- Kids entertainer (for the insane only);*
- Kitchen fitter;*
- Light removals;*
- Locksmith;*

- Mechanic (mobile);*
- Musician/entertainer;*
- Odd jobs;*
- Oven cleaner (mobile);*
- Painter/decorator;*
- Patio cleaner;*
- Photographer;*
- Piano tuner;
- Plasterer;*
- Plumber;
- Private chauffeur;
- Private investigator;*
- Private teacher;
- Psychic (but you should know this already!);*
- Seamstress;*
- Surveyor;
- Taxi driver;
- Tow bar fitter;*
- Travel agent;
- Tree surgeon;
- Vet;
- Web designer;*
- Wedding/|event organizer;*
- Will writer;*
- Window cleaner.*

**Part Service/Part Sales Businesses**
- Burger Van;
- Caravan site;*

- Fence maker/erector;*
- Florist;*
- Foil blocking;*
- Hire Business (ladders, trailers, pedalos, anything!);*
- Hotel/B&B;*
- Mobile nappy supplies;*
- Picture framing;*
- Post office;
- Printer (screen, letterpress, litho, digi);*
- Pub landlord;
- Restaurant/café;
- Sandwiches/catering;*
- Security alarm fitter/supplier;*
- Takeaway (pizzas, kebabs etc.);*
- TV aerial/dish fitter/supplier;*
- Undertakers.

## Sales Based Businesses
- All retail;
- Car Sales;*
- Importers;*
- Ice cream sales;*
- Internet sales (ebay etc.);*
- Mail order sales;*
- Market trader;*
- Second-hand goods (washing machines, baby items etc.).*

## Production/Manufacturing
- Bakers;
- Bee Keeper;

- Chocolatier;*
- Plastic Fabricators;*
- Sign Makers;*
- Stain glass artisan;*
- Vacuum Forming;*
- Window Makers/Fitters.

**Unearned Income**

- Author;*
- Property Rental;*
- Stock Market Trading.*

Of course the above lists are only a few examples of the many possibilities available, some of which you may need qualifications or licenses for and others not (marked* above). For a more comprehensive list, pick up the Yellow Pages.

But from the business management point of view a service is a service and a sale is a sale and it makes little difference what service you are providing or what goods you are selling, business wise they all work the same and a good *net* profit is the aim of them all. Although of course they all have their individual plus/minus points which you'll need to look into before commitment. But at the end of the day you need to find a business that:

- You enjoy;
- You are able to do;
- Is profitable enough for your needs;
- You have adequate finances to operate;
- Preferably can be run from home (which we'll discuss shortly).

And remember this has nothing to do with intelligence or qualifications etc. *Everybody*, from any background can do *something* which somebody else will pay for, even if it's only cleaning or digging holes! And there's certainly nothing belittling about either of these, in fact multimillion pound businesses have been built on both. So don't go making excuses!

## Service Based vs. Sales Based

Initially it's likely that you'll either operate a service business or a sales business (or combination).

If you are operating a service based business obviously your only income will be generated from the fees that you charge which will be on an hourly or daily rate or a fixed price for the job.

The downside to this type of business is that your top earnings will generally be limited by the amount of hours in a week (less your overheads). So consequently few service providers get rich, but most make a good living and less go bankrupt.

However, if you are fortunate enough to generate more business than you can handle personally, don't turn it away, farm it out to an associate. This is basically what I did with the driving school. I started as a sole trader then as business increased (due to hard work and good service); I took on more instructors who worked in their own cars (under my name) on a subcontracting basis, meaning that they were working for me but not *employed* by me *per se.*

Basically, they paid me a weekly fee and I provided them with business. Doing this I built up to 12 cars over a number of years. And furthermore I was then able to sell the business (which is still running successfully) as a good going concern. All I was selling was good will, but as it was built up over a 30 year period with an unrivalled reputation this was worth a lot of money.

Also as a result of the driving school income I was able to enter the property rental market and ultimately *retire* early.

Another excellent thing about the service industry is that in most cases you can easily avoid business premises, thus reducing overheads and thereby increasing net profits.

If you want to get into sales, it's more likely that you'll need business premises and thereby higher costs, but not necessarily, especially if you decide to go into mail order/internet sales or even markets. But of course an immediate disadvantage of sales is that in most cases you will have to buy and hold stock, which takes up space, so think carefully about what you want to sell – selling watches is going to take up far less space than selling wardrobes!

Another downside to being in sales is that your turnover will need to be higher and you will therefore possibly be required to register for VAT which is a particularly nasty club that you are better off out of, but we'll come onto this later.

## Training Programs

You've probably seen numerous adverts offering to extract your money in exchange for various 'certified' tuition courses. Some may well be genuine but many will leave you in debt with either a worthless qualification or nothing.

This sort of trickery is rife in the Driving Instructor industry where it's possible to pay £3,000 or more in advance with only a very small chance of qualifying. What they don't tell you clearly is that there's only a 28% pass rate for the final exam and you only get three attempts. And very often the training is inadequate, substandard and/or badly timed.

I've written a guide about qualifying as a Driving Instructor without risking thousands of pounds. No doubt similar low cost advice is available for just about every occupation, so do your homework, look around and *never* pay large sums in advance. Even if the training establishment is good and genuine, if they go bust the day after you've paid them, you've lost the lot!

And remember that more often than not it's the large *glossy brochure* businesses that are the worst. Don't trust anyone - this must sound cynical, but it comes from a life time of experience!

## Buying an existing Business

Even if you intend starting your own business from scratch it could be worth looking into an existing going concern if for no other reason than to gain some information and study the accounts. You may even find that this is the way forward for you.

Daltons Weekly is a good place to start looking, but make sure you know exactly what you are buying and that the present owner signs a statement that he/she will not start up in competition with you within a certain distance and/or time.

Needless to say, if you go this route, never pay anywhere near the asking price and always have legal representation.

And don't let them kid you that so much of the income is not declared in the accounts - this may or may not be the case, but if the business is not making a reasonable *net* profit as per several years accounts, then it's not worth buying.

## Franchises

Most franchises require large cash up front payments and then an ongoing percentage fee. Some of these are positively dubious, but contrarily some are ok, so they all need careful judgement according to their merits.

Just in case you don't know; a franchise is an arrangement where a person or company establishes a successful business concept in a particular area and then sells or rents the rights to use the same name/profile and concept in another selected area(s). There could be, and usually are several franchisees connected to each franchise.

Probably the most well known franchises include:

- MacDonald's;

- Pizza Hut;

- Subway;

- Kentucky Fried Chicken;

- BSM & AA Driving Instructors etc.

But there are literally thousands of others large and small. Check the Daltons Weekly for more info: http://www.daltons.co.uk.

The advantage theoretically is that you could have an instant established business, but of course this comes at a price and it's not forced to be successful anyway. The only thing that is guaranteed is that the franchisee (you) will end up parting with a large sum of money which could make you bankrupt!

Before even considering a franchise you would be wise to speak to many existing franchisees. And thoroughly scrutinise the company's claims and terms of contract. But my advice is; stay clear, you don't need them!

## Partnerships

If you feel you must enter a partnership, make sure that everything is clearly down in writing and signed, even if it's your best friend. And this must include exactly who is responsible for what.

More partnerships fail than succeed - enough said.

## Starting up Abroad

For some inexplicable reason many individuals and couples who have had no prior business experience think that they can run a successful business (usually a bar/restaurant) in a country where they don't even speak the language - just because the sun is shining! Clearly they live in cloud cuckoo land!

Several years ago we owned a property in Spain and seriously considered buying a business out there. While we were looking we saw many expats who were desperate to sell up and return to the UK. Often they were underfinanced, or simply didn't know what they were doing and in many cases were working long hours in the soaring heat for virtually nothing or even at a loss - such was their dream! Even sadder, others were desperate to sell up due to illness or death of a spouse.

Even if you do have business experience, you'll find that when working abroad you will not be on a level playing field. Basically the local business people want it all for themselves and will make it as awkward as possible for you to survive. And of course your only chance of doing any business will be with other expats unless you speak the lingo and have thoroughly integrated into their society.

I've personally run a sign business in Cyprus specialising in magnetic vehicle signs. Even this was hard despite my experience and being the only magnetic sign supplier on the island.

Australia, New Zealand, Canada and the USA are exceptions to the above, where you'll no doubt be welcome as long as you meet their stringent immigration criteria. But if you can't make it in the UK, you've absolutely no chance in a non English speaking country.

# Gross Profit & Net Profit

One of the reasons that some sole traders fail is simply because they inadvertently get their *net profit* mixed up with their *gross profit* or *turnover* and start spending money that isn't theirs. We'll now make this clear.

### Turnover

Your annual turnover is the total income from all sales and/or services in the year regardless of what goes out. If for instance you are paid for labour and materials, both are considered as income/turnover even though you may use part of this immediately to buy materials.

Turnover has nothing to do with profit. You could have a £10 million pound turnover and still make a substantial net loss - in fact many do!

If your business is *service* based you turnover will be much lower than a *sales* based business and in this case will also be your *gross profit*.

### Gross Profit

Gross Profit (GP) applies *to sales and production* based businesses and is the difference between the buying/production price of your goods and the selling price.

For instance if you were selling shoes and you buy a pair wholesale for £20 and then sell them for £50, your gross profit (GP) would be £30, or percentage wise this equates to 60% (sale price less purchase price divided by sale price times 100):

| | | |
|---|---|---|
| Sale Price | £50.00 | less |
| Cost Price | £20.00 | |
| Gross Profit | £30.00 | divided by |
| Sale Price | £50.00 | x 100 |
| **Gross Profit** | **60%** | |

This is fairly simple when dealing with a pair of shoes, but the amount of caterers who haven't got a clue what their GP is, is astonishing.

You may have seen the recent TV series 'The Hotel Inspector'. This series has shown several supposedly 'intelligent' people selling meals *en masse* for a virtual loss and not even being aware of it! Then they can't understand why they go bust!

Whereas the major breweries and pub chains are very stringent about their GP requirements as they *know* the significance. You need to know the cost price of every item on the plate right down to the last chip or disaster will follow! And remember the gross profit doesn't include the cost of cooking the meal or other overhead expenses which we'll look at now.

## Overhead Expenses

Overhead expenses apply to all types of businesses, service, sales and production and are the expenses incurred in running the business excluding the cost of sales.

These come into two categories for tax purposes; *Revenue* expenses and *Capital* expenses

Revenue Expenses include:

- Rent/rates;
- Mortgage interest;
- Advertising;
- Wages;
- Decorations and general repairs to premises;
- Computer software;
- Computer maintenance;
- Cleaning premises (interior and windows);
- Utilities for premises (gas, electric, water etc.);
- Telephone and internet (including mobile);
- Bank charges/credit card merchant fees;
- Printing, stationery, office supplies etc.;
- Postage;

- Insurance (property, vehicles, public liability etc.);
- Fuel (for business use);
- Maintenance of vehicles;
- Legal and professional (solicitors/accountants);
- Commissions to agents/sub contractors.

Capital Expenses include:

- Depreciation of vehicles (or percentage of);
- Depreciation of machinery;
- Depreciation of computers;
- Depreciation of office furnishings;
- Cost of office fixtures/fittings;
- Legal costs of buying/selling property;
- Property improvements/renovations;
- Mortgage redemption charges etc.

I'll explain the difference between capital and revenue expenses under the taxation heading.

**Net Profit**

The net profit is the gross profit less the revenue overhead expenses and the capital allowances on the capital expenses and is the amount that you would ultimately then have to pay income tax on. Frightening isn't it?

So, the higher the gross profit is and the lower the overhead expenses are, the more *you* will end up with! And for this reason I personally have avoided using business premises since the café (which was many years ago) and also would never employ staff. In many cases this can mean the difference between survival and failure. If you spend £10k or more per year on premises that you don't need, this amount effectively comes directly off your *net* profit, i.e. out of your pocket!

You need the gap between *turnover* and *net profit* to be as small as possible and then you should also be able to keep out of VAT which will be very much to your advantage, which we'll talk about later.

You may think that you can't expand this way, which to a point maybe true, but I've seen too many good individuals go bankrupt as a result of getting this wrong.

## Tweaking GP's and Overheads

By increasing GP and lowering overheads it's easily possible to increase the *net* profit without altering the turnover. Assuming a turnover of £100k, a GP of 60% and overheads of £35k you will see that the net profit is £25k.

| | |
|---|---|
| Sale Price | £100,000.00 |
| GP | £60,000.00 |
| Overheads | £35,000.00 |
| **Net Profit** | **£25,000.00** |

Notice that without altering the turnover, if the GP was increased by 5% (by increasing sale prices) and the overheads were reduced by 10% (by various means) the net profit would increase to £33,500.

| | |
|---|---|
| Sale Price | £100,000.00 |
| GP | £65,000.00 |
| Overheads | £31,500.00 |
| **Net Profit** | **£33,500.00** |

Conversely, if the GP was lowered 5% and the overheads increased by 10% the net profit would reduce to £16,500.

| | |
|---|---|
| Sale Price | £100,000.00 |
| GP | £55,000.00 |
| Overheads | £38,500.00 |
| **Net Profit** | **£16,500.00** |

See how delicate it all is? And how important it is to ensure the highest GP possible and the lowest overheads!

Obviously all this is hypothetical and it could be argued (and may of course happen) that by reducing GP you may increase turnover and possibly the *net* profit, but you would also be working harder! It's a balancing act that you can only get right through a certain amount of trial and error.

**Mark ups**

A different and probably an easier way of looking at GP's is by 'mark ups'. For instance if you buy an item for £1 and sell it for £3 the mark up is 3 : 1, (67% GP), or if you buy for £1 and sell for £10 then the mark up is 10 : 1 (90% GP). This is very important as if you want to survive your very minimum mark up should be 3 : 1, with the possible exception of very high priced items like cars etc.

If you attempt to operate with less than a 3 : 1 mark up I guarantee that you will fail, and even 3 : 1 is painfully slim as you'll see shortly. I personally wouldn't entertain less than a 10 : 1 mark up and this is nothing to do with greed - just survival! Remember that all your other overhead expenses have to be taken into consideration before you end up with a profit and advertising alone will probably account for 50% of the sale price and other overheads at least 10%.

Here are a few examples to compare:

**5: 1 Mark Up - 80% GP**

| | | |
|---|---|---|
| Sale Price | £30.00 | less |
| Purchase Price | £6.00 | |
| Advertising | £15.00 | |
| Other Overheads | £3.00 | |
| **Net Profit** | **£6.00** | |

**3: 1 Mark Up - 67% GP**

| | | |
|---|---|---|
| Sale Price | £30.00 | less |
| Purchase Price | £10.00 | |
| Advertising | £15.00 | |
| Other Overheads | £3.00 | |
| **Net Profit** | **£2.00** | |

**10: 1 Mark Up - 90% GP**

| | | |
|---|---|---|
| Sale Price | £30.00 | less |
| Purchase Price | £3.00 | |
| Advertising | £15.00 | |
| Other Overheads | £3.00 | |
| **Net Profit** | **£9.00** | |

Obviously the above are purely hypothetical and I know that you can twist figures round to say virtually anything, but it's nonetheless a good formula to follow - ignore it at your peril!

### The Perfect Product

The closer you can get to a 100% GP the better. Information guides, music, games or software sold via instant downloads achieves exactly this, and once the work has been produced you are effectively selling nothing and this could be operated from anywhere in the world!

Collectively we all know everything and this is because *individually* we all know something different - what do you know?

I've written guides about what I know:

- Sign Making;
- Driving Instructing;
- Self Employment;
- Music (keyboard improvisation);
- Cyprus Living;
- Traded Options;
- Buy to Let Properties;
- Making Magnetic Business Cards;
- Relaxation techniques using Binaural Beats.

These have taken me quite some time to produce, but now certainly has proved worthwhile. Why don't you write about what you know? This could then be sold as an eBook on line (via your own website), or Kindle, iBookstore, Google books, Kobo, Nook etc. - or produced into paperback via http://www.lulu.com for pennies! - Anyone can do it!

Every single person is unique in the fact that we all have different experiences and this is our part in the evolution of consciousness, that's why we're here! And whether you think your life has been blessed or damned, I guarantee that you know something that someone will pay you for.

For instance have you:

- Survived prison?
- Been homeless?
- Lived with incontinence or had a colostomy?
- Lived on a canal barge?
- Caught the biggest fish in the lake?
- Beaten cancer or any other disease?
- Trained a chicken to lay square eggs?
- The list is endless!

And remember you don't have to be the world's greatest expert on what you write about, you just need to know more than 50% of the population do about a particular topic - it's not rocket science!

With the technology available today, anyone can produce a quality guide on a PC via MS Word. And don't get too hung up about 'grammar'. My guides are probably riddled with grammatical errors, but to be honest, do you care? The chances are that your grammar is no better than mine, so you probably won't even notice!

Over the years I have spent hundreds of pounds buying information guides and software on various topics, most of which has been downloaded at little or no cost to the seller, but it's also been very worthwhile to me. A double winner, they make money and I'm happy!

With all of my books, guides and recordings (this one included) I always aimed to give *much more* in 'use value' to the recipient than I receive in payment. And this is good business practice, the reason for which will become clear as we continue.

If self publishing interests you, I would suggest that looking at http://www.lulu.com is a good starting point as they will give you free ISBN numbers and the 'MS Word' templates enabling you to produce a book for print or ePub.

Kindle use a different format called 'Mobi', but having produced your book in the ePub format, this can then easily be reformatted for Mobi.

I will shortly be writing a guide with full instructions about the various formats available and how to create them easily. So if you are interested in this, keep an eye on my website.

# Business Premises & Staff

If your business needs premises, you must be aware that the cost of this will drastically reduce your net profit and this can often make the difference between solvency and bankruptcy. Having said this of course the nature of some businesses make premises and probably staff essential.

## Business Premises

Ok, so assuming you must have premises, remember you will be paying:

- Rent (or mortgage);
- Business rates;
- Utilities on the premises;
- Probably staff;
- Cleaning (inside and out);
- Furnishings/fittings;
- Insurance (property);
- Redecorations/maintenance etc.

Having paid all this out another point to consider is that *most* of these expenses won't increase if you use your premises 24 hours per day.

Many restaurants for instance open at 7:00pm and close at 11:00pm or 12:00 meaning that they are paying 100% rent/rates for only 25% or less of the time.

By contrast MacDonald's open their doors to catch the breakfast trade as well as the takeaways and late night eaters. A restaurant near us called 'Taybarns' does similar and also has those irritating crane machines installed where you put in a pound to try and win a 10p 'meerkat' with about a 500 - 1 chance of success - a definite winner from the business point of view, as idiots continually fill them up with money - a point to remember!

In the café that we had (a long time ago) we had a high pay out fruit machine that was installed on a 50/50 basis by the supplier. Our share of the profits almost paid the property rent on a regular basis!

When starting a new business, make sure that the premises has the necessary planning consent for *your* business. Contact your local council for more information.

Sometime ago I knew a chap who'd just bought a shop premises to open a takeaway, but was shocked when the consent was continually refused on the grounds of inadequate parking, despite the fact that there were other takeaways in the same block with the same problem. I must admit that I can't understand why this happened, but it's a point that you must be aware of.

### Staff

I know that for some businesses employing staff is essential and can't be avoided, but in case you've not already figured it out my personal view is to keep things as simple as possible and employ no one except on a self employed basis.

Obviously employing staff may increase your overheads to a large degree (and consequently decrease your net profit). And remember they will need paying even at times when there is no business being generated and also for their holidays (a luxury which you won't receive yourself).

Apart from this they will also be eligible for paid maternity leave, and if you don't employ some-one because you think they might be pregnant, they could sue you for discrimination. And if you look at them the wrong way or (heaven forbid) make the wrong sort of joke, they could sue you for sexual or racial or homophobic harassment. And then of course it will cost you if you have to make them redundant.

As an employed person you may think that all these rules are fine, but when you seriously consider running your own business, you'll realise how pathetic and damaging they are!

And even worse you will also be an unpaid tax collector sorting out their PAYE and they'll probably sue you if you get it wrong. And because your turnover will have to be fairly high in order to employ them, you will not be able to avoid registering for VAT - more unpaid paper work, which we'll talk about later!

It's a minefield - do you really want to go there?

The only time I actually employed anyone was when we had the café - and she robbed us blind, big time - I learned my lesson. And of course every pound stolen comes directly off your *net* profit - out of your pocket!

If you must employ staff, you're better off with part timers which will enable you to arrange adequate staff at the busy times and less at other times. But remember that they are human beings with their own dreams and aspirations which should never be discouraged and should be treat fairly and honestly at all times.

Finally, make sure that the terms and conditions are clearly written into a contract of employment and signed/witnessed by both parties.

# Business Successes & Failures

Following are a few examples of some successes/failures and the reasons why.

**Example 1**

Many years ago (in the early 70's) I worked in a small cabaret club as a musician. This was a new business in a prime position with private parking in the centre of Sheffield.

The owner was an experienced businessman with a string of successful small shops - no fool! It was always his dream to open a cabaret club/restaurant. He spent thousands of pounds refurbishing the premises; employed a 'top' chef at great expense; employed a resident trio (of which I was a part); plus regular guest acts. Of course he also had an advertising campaign in the local papers and radio. No expenses were spared and he appeared to be doing everything right.

The idea was to attract a high class of clientele for expensive dining and drinking in an up market environment. As the premises had a 'restaurant' license, customers could legally drink alcohol into the early hours as long as they had eaten a meal. And a great deal of the potential profit was based on the alcohol sales.

But think of the overheads he had:

- Top chef, plus assistant, plus other kitchen staff;
- 5 waitresses;
- 3 Band members;
- 3 barmen, 1 doorman;
- Guest cabaret acts;
- 2 cleaners;
- Advertising;
- Premises costs (including utilities);
- Laundry (table clothes/napkins etc.);
- Food/drinks (cost of sales).

All this had to be paid for out of the GP from the food and drinks before he could start recouping any of his original investment costs and begin making a *net* profit. It was of course a calculated gamble.

I don't know whether you remember the 70's or not, but it was a particularly bad time for Sheffield. Not long after this business started; petrol prices started going up literally every day and trebled in the year. Inflation went rampant and Sheffield's steel works (the life blood of the city) started closing down, followed by the coal mines in surrounding areas. You may have seen the film 'The Full Monty' which showed Sheffield at this time.

Needless to say all of this didn't do the business any good and he was losing money at a colossal rate. And on top of this, the chef was bleeding him dry by wasting huge amounts of expensive stock as well as giving it away.

But this guy was a fighter; he realised that his dream wasn't going to come to fruition, so he changed tactics. He sacked the chef and brought in a group of strippers. To get round the licensing law, he charged an entrance fee and gave everyone chicken and chips whether they wanted it or not. This resulted in the place becoming jammed packed every night and the business started making a profit. It was no doubt a different type of clientele (or at least they didn't bring their wives) and certainly not what he'd originally intended.

From my point of view it was all quite amusing. From the stage all that could be seen was hundreds of ogling faces with tongues hanging out and the rear view of the strippers! To supplement the strippers' wages and for a bit of a laugh we (the band) used to auction off what they'd taken off. So some poor sod would end up going home pissed out of his brains with a pair of sweaty knickers in his pocket that he'd just paid about £50 for!

Anyway, to cut a long story short, the local council were not happy that he was getting round the licensing law so blatantly, and were determined to close the business down. As they couldn't get him on the licensing laws, they managed to close him down for obscene acts, after the police were in the front row every night for about three months 'gathering evidence'! Our guitarist had the job of asking the girls what they were going to do and to tell them that they shouldn't do anything obscene - the only trouble was that he didn't fully understand the meaning of *obscene!*

It was such a shame as the owner was genuinely a good honest man and at the end was a good profitable business, which basically gave people what they wanted (despite whether you happen to agree with it or not), and surprisingly there was never any trouble there ever. Had the same business been open today, no-one would bat an eyelid and they'd probably even let kids in (well maybe not), but things were different then!

The moral of this example is: Even if you do everything apparently right, you're still not forced to succeed and never forget that you could be a victim of circumstances due to bad timing (or something else).

## Example 2

This next example was a driving school with the crazy idea that they could teach anyone to drive in a week under the title of 'intensive courses'.

Their adverts even guaranteed success and the fee was based on a two hour assessment. Having taken the initial assessment lesson, the fee which guaranteed them to pass, was then payable in full in advance. The test was then applied for (this was before the days of the theory test) and one week before the test day, the intensive course began.

Having received all the fees in advance, the instructors could then scream and shout at the pupils with no fear of them going elsewhere as they'd already paid in full and a refund was totally out of the question.

On the day of the test, most were embarrassingly inadequate and some were too frightened to even go through with the humiliation, in which case they lost their right to any further 'free' tuition. And of course the majority who did go through with it failed miserably and were then given 'free' tuition when the school decided to fit them in and this continued until the pupil got so disillusioned that they finally packed up or cut their losses and went elsewhere.

The few that did actually pass were usually youngsters with good aptitudes who would have passed with less lessons anyway had they taken the conventional route.

Due to the way this business was operated a huge amount of business was generated quickly with only a few pupils (remember each one was having maybe 40 lessons in a week). So this enabled the business to expand to several cars very quickly. But as the business had no foundation and was built on lies and deceit, it went bankrupt within a year owing huge amounts for advertising and advance payments taken from unsuspecting clients even up to the day before insolvency.

The moral of this example is: Don't tell lies, don't spend fees that you haven't earned and don't make promises that you can't keep.

The only way this business could have kept going was to keep expanding by using more and more advance payments for wages and for overheads etc., but invariably the bubble must burst. A one car driving school with 40 pupils taking one lesson a week builds a solid foundation and is far stronger than a 6 car school with 6 pupils each having 40 lessons in one week.

Similar methods are used by off plan foreign property developers (Spain and Cyprus to mention two); they often take large advance payments to pay off what they owe on the previous developments and hope that people keep buying so that they can then pay for the present one before they go bust!

And as you may well know, in both Spain and Cyprus the recent property crash has caused countless insolvencies!

## Example 3

Back in the boom days of the 80's a couple of friends of mine had a really profitable sign making business (just the two of them). They rented modest premises, but as business increased they felt the need to employ some help. In order to pay for the additional help, they needed to increase trade further and therefore needed larger premises and more machinery to deal with this, then more staff, and then more business etc., etc.

By the time they'd finished all this; they had increased their turnover enormously, were committed to a long term lease on the new premises, had a huge loan for new equipment and had to keep things moving at the same level just to pay the wages bill. But their *net* profit had hardly gone up at all!

Then the good times ended, business started slowing down; their customers were demanding lower prices and longer credit terms; they started having to make staff redundant; then they couldn't pay the rent or loans and consequently they went bust and lost their houses (which they foolishly used as collateral for various loans).

Ok, they might have made a fortune, but clearly something went badly wrong. Basically they got too big too quick. It's often the case that the quicker a business builds up, the quicker it falls down.

Their failure incidentally was nothing to do with the quality of their work which was excellent; it was simply down to bad accounting and greed!

And the moral of this example is: 'If it aint broke don't fix it!'

## Example 4

This next example was the company who I employed to produce my roof signs (for my driving school supplies business).

This company did vacuum forming and very well. They rented a large industrial unit near Worksop and employed several workers. Their biggest customer was the coal board as they made ABS containers which were used to attach to machinery to bring the coal out of the mines. They had continual large orders for these containers and were constantly under pressure to deliver faster. For fear of losing the orders, they took out a huge loan for two new large vacuum forming machines.

Then the mines shut down, they lost the orders and didn't have enough other business to pay their loans, wages and overheads, so consequently went bust!

The moral of this example is: 'Never put all your eggs in one basket!' Although this business was honest, trustworthy and capable, they also made a similar mistake to example 2 in the fact that they expanded without a solid customer foundation - having lots of small customers is far better than one or two big ones, then no-one can hold you to ransom!

## Example 5

You'll be pleased to know that this next example is a success story.

Back in the 80's/90's, I was running both the driving school and the driving school supplies business concurrently and consequently my wife and I had long busy days. Several times a week we would eat out quite late both to simply 'eat' and to unwind. Our favourite restaurant was run by an Italian guy and his wife. We'll call him Nemo but this wasn't actually his name.

Nemo was a hairdresser by day and chef by night, a real grafter, but what made his business so successful was that he had exactly the right balance and operated as follows:

- He had the right sized restaurant, not so many tables that he couldn't cope with, but large enough to ensure a decent profit;

- He didn't waste money on unnecessary staff. Mid week the place was run by just him and his wife (he cooked, she served). Then at busy periods he took on an extra part time waiter and a kitchen assistant;

- The food was excellent and he and his wife created a warm and welcoming atmosphere - certainly one of our all time favourite restaurants;

- He owned the premises;

- After a few years of successful trading, he sold the business but retained the freehold of the property, then concentrated on his hairdressing for a few years before selling that also;

- After a respectable time period he opened another restaurant in a different part of town under a new name;

To my knowledge he did this four times with restaurants and three times with hairdressers, each time retaining the freehold properties.

In short he'd got exactly the right winning formula and knew how to maximize the profit at the same time as building a property portfolio with guaranteed rents. And as he was never desperate to sell, he could always hold out for the best prices.

He also kept out of VAT (we'll discuss this later).

# Finance

Banks and accountants are both essential to a certain degree, but can also become an unnecessary drain on your overheads if you're not very careful and watch them vigilantly.

## Banks

Needless to say, you will need a bank account, but if you rush off to your bank and tell them that you are going to start a business they will inevitably try and sell you all sorts of *helpful* services that you probably don't need and charge you for these accordingly. Never forget that banks are money making machines and will ruthlessly pursue their aim without blinking an eyelid at making you bankrupt if you default on a loan. And they're all the same!

If you can manage it, the best type to have is the normal *no fees, no frills* personal account which they wouldn't allow you to have for business purposes, but if you trade under your own name and don't bother telling them, they wouldn't have any reason to know or object!

If you trade under a different name of course this would not be possible, in which case you would have to do your homework and find the best deal, but remember they all have nasty hidden charges for various services that you may inadvertently sign up for. Some charge a fixed monthly fee, others will charge per transaction and these can be substantial (over a 12 month period).

When I was running the driving school alongside the sign business, I had three accounts; one for each business and one for personal use. At the end of one tax year when checking my accounts, I noticed that the fees charged by the two business accounts, the credit card merchant account and the accountant combined, was actually more than my mortgage payments. Most of these fees were sneaked in here and there, not appearing to be very much individually, but accumulatively they were substantial.

The next day I closed both business accounts and sacked the accountant thereby reducing my overheads and increasing my net profit accordingly.

## Credit Card Merchant Fees

There's absolutely no doubt about it that most businesses need the facility to accept payments via credit/debit cards. When I first offered this facility for my sign business, my turnover increased dramatically. If you run a *sales* based business with a shop premises, you will obviously need to have a chip and pin machine and pay the relevant merchant fees, which will probably be a minimum monthly fee plus a usage percentage. When I had the sign business these fees weren't too bad, but I know they've increased a lot since which is why I no longer use them.

A superb low cost alternative is paypal which is what I use now. No doubt you know that paypal is mainly used via ebay for internet sales. But it can also be used for telephone sales via any credit/debit card even if the user doesn't have a paypal account. As the fees are quite high, you must gear this cost into the sale price. But the really good thing is that there are no monthly charges - you pay per transaction and can choose a percentage structure according to the price of your goods. See: http://www.paypal.com for more details.

There are also similar alternatives such as http://www.nochex.com, https://www.braintreepayments.com, http://www.google.co.uk/wallet etc., but they all have their individual pros and cons, so check which is best for you.


## Finance

Whatever business you are into, it's likely that you will need to buy machinery, stock or a vehicle etc., and may need finance for this. My advice is to borrow as little as you can get away with and look around for the best deal.

Most banks now have hidden extra charges that never used to exist such as arrangement fees, monthly overdraft fees and early redemption charges. Make sure you know and understand the terms of the contract (including and especially the small print), and make sure that the reason you're taking it is going to increase your income, otherwise there's no point. And finally think long and hard before using your house as security, it's more often the *second charges* that cause repossessions.

I was once in the situation where I was buying in pre cut vinyl lettering for my sign business at the rate of £400 per month. I sensibly borrowed £4000 over 12 months to buy my own pre cut lettering machine, which maintained the status quo for a year and then subsequently increased my net profit considerably.

Try and avoid overdrafts as these can be outrageously expensive (especially unarranged ones). Have an overdraft facility by all means but try and avoid using it. At the time of writing this, the bank lending rate is/was 0.5%, yet some banks are charging 19% for an arranged overdraft. This is just one of the many devious tricks the banks play.

It baffles me how many individuals and businesses have an overdraft facility that they *just* manage to keep below on a regular basis, and of course pay interest accordingly. Surely if they can do this, they could just as easily *just* keep in credit and pocket the interest.

Curiously the government manages to make the same mistake and the bottom line is that every man, woman and child in Britain is nearly £80,000 in debt as a result of incompetent government. So if the IMF interest rate increases to 5%, each one of us will need to pay (via taxation) £4,000 per year in interest alone just to service this debt before paying anything off the capital - frightening!

### Accountants

Using the services of a good accountant is essential when you first start out and probably for some years. As always, shop around, but depending on the type of business and the work involved the fees could vary considerably. A good accountant should save you money. You need one who can make $2 + 2 =$ whatever is most convenient for you, and surprisingly most deliver!

But just because you have an accountant doesn't mean that you don't need to be involved with your accounts. You will still need to prepare these. The accountant will then verify and improve them, but he/she must have something to work with!

How to prepare your accounts will be dealt with later.

# Advertising/Marketing

Advertising is the life blood of every business and will almost certainly be the greatest overhead expense. Effective advertising will generate business or sales and ultimately increase your *net* profit. But of course overpriced or ineffective advertising is money down the drain, so choose carefully and make sure that you keep records of which advertising *is* the most effective.

Anyway, what type of advertising you need will be determined by your choice of business, but you will probably need a combination of some of the following:

- Shop premises (inc. 'A' boards);
- Vehicle signs;
- Newspapers (national/local);
- Magazines;
- Direct mail;
- Internet/Website;
- Video;
- Online auction sites;
- Yellow Pages;
- Word of mouth/recommendations;
- Leaflets;
- Shop windows adverts;
- Discounts, Special Offers & Freebies;
- Advertising gifts;
- Exhibitions/Trade Fairs;
- Stationery/business cards etc.;
- Company logo/Profile;
- Xmas/birthday cards.

## Shop Premises

If your business demands that you have premises, make sure that you maximize the cost of this expenditure, by displaying a good quality fascia sign (illuminated is best and essential if you are open after dark).

Depending on the type of business incorporate an attractive window display and/or window and door lettering if appropriate. A pavement 'A' board could also be used to display any special offers etc.

If you have a café with outside seating; note that the aluminium chairs/tables look far better (even after 10 years) than the cheap plastic ones. The banner type dividers with your business name and logo over printed also help create a good impression for a low initial investment.

And remember that it's not just flies that are attracted by bright lights and colour - flags/bunting and balloons work in a similar way.

Finally make sure that your windows, doors and fascia are always clean inside and out, remembering that your premises is an advert 24/7 even when you are closed!

## Vehicle Signs

Whatever business you run, you will almost certainly have a vehicle (car or van). If you use a van, have it sign written with PVC lettering/logos/graphics. But if you only have a car and use this also for personal use, the instantly removable magnetic door and rear panel signs are the answer. These are very low cost and after the initial small investment, will be free advertising and believe me it works!

But make sure that you get the message across effectively remembering that you may only be seen for a few seconds, so make the phone number as BIG as possible! Look at the following:

**Burt Lancaster**
**Chimney Sweep**
All Areas Covered
**Tel 0114 364 3333**

**CHIMNEY SWEEP**
**364 3333**

I think you'll agree that the first sign looks more artistic and professional, but the second one will bring you more business guaranteed! Or of course you could do something in between, but remember how important the phone number is.

## Newspapers (national/local)

Newspaper adverts (national or local) can be an excellent advertising media, but you must make sure that it's effective and value for money, remembering that they are dead and in the bin the next day.

When I had the driving school, I used a very short (2 lines) classified advert in the Sheffield Star every day for 30 years - and it worked. At times as a test I doubled the size of the advert and it didn't alter the response - just the price. You only need the entry and the people who are interested will find you!

As with the sign, make it as brief and to the point as possible. My adverts read: 'Pass in a Mini - Martin 328188' in the driving school column. Had I put: 'Pass your test in a Mini', it would have said no more but would have gone into another line and cost substantially more (over the year).

Never let the canvassers sell you a blank line above and below your advert to 'make it stand out', this will just double the price. You will be paying for paper *and* ink, make sure you get both!

Finally always check *circulation* figures NOT *readership* figures, many are simply not value for money. And of course if you run a local business, there's no point in advertising in a national newspaper, but I'm sure you're not stupid.

## Magazines

These are an excellent media for mail order sales and unlike newspapers have a much longer lifespan - they get passed around and can eventually end up in the doctors' waiting rooms for months!

Obviously you must choose the magazine carefully and again look into *circulation* figures, although their readership figures will probably contain an element of truth.

For my driving school supplies business (which was national by mail order), I used quarter page adverts in trade magazines (aimed exclusively at Driving Schools) and these were very effective.

However, if possible ensure a right hand page. The top right hand quarter of a right hand page is the best position by far and don't let anyone try and convince you otherwise, this is a proven fact, and if you have to, pay extra to get this position.

**Direct Mail**

Similar to trade or special interest magazines, direct mail can be a very effective medium especially if you want to pinpoint your campaign to a specific group of people.

You will need to get an up to date mailing list with no duplications which are available from http://www.hilitedms.co.uk for a variety of interests. You can either buy the names out right (for using repeatedly) or rent the names for one time use only. Once you have secured your own customers (from any media), these can then be stored in a data base as *your* mailing list which *you* can then sell or rent out!

The downside to direct mail is that it can be very labour intensive (stuffing envelopes) and expensive - the cost of the printing, buying envelopes and mailing.

This was my first choice when I started the driving school supplies business, but then mailing lists weren't so readily available for driving schools, so I literally copied them all out from all the Yellow Pages nationwide (from the library) which was very time consuming.

The main reason I chose this method was because there was a free offer on through the Post Office for a 1000 mailing which of course saved me all the postage costs. Anyway the bottom line was that it worked and I repeated it again successfully at the full cost. This helped me to become established and then I continued with the trade magazines which were just as effective but less labour intensive.

Check with the Post Office to see what offers are available, as they alter from time to time.

**Website**

In this day and age just about every business needs a website of some description, but do remember that in most cases you will need other advertising to direct your clients to your site.

Sure you could be found via the internet search engines and you should maximize this as much as possible, but I wouldn't rely on it too much unless you really know what you are doing or pay someone to do it for you.

Having someone design, produce and maintain your website could be expensive, especially if you choose the wrong company and even then will not guarantee that you will be found by the search engines. So my advice is that you create your own as I have done, or research any prospective design company very carefully - it's a jungle out there!

My websites were created (by me) using serif software which costs about £60 (see: http://www.serif.com). Alternatively you could use one of the free site builders: - Joomla or Wordpress. Both are excellent.

Ok mine might not be the best websites on the block, but I think you'll agree that they are more than adequate - and that's all they have to be! I'm certainly not a computer whizz, but I managed to do this without too much hassle and fairly easily.

But remember, the '*look*' of the site is nowhere near as important as the '*search-ability*' and for this you must study SEO (search engine optimisation). A super duper lights flashing, bells ringing website might look great, but if you're the only one who ever sees it, it aint gonna do you much good! And believe me there are too many companies out there who will produce this rot for you and relieve you of a fortune!

From the 'search engines' point of view a plain site with no fancy fonts or graphics is best, and will more likely be 'found' - but there's also much more to it than that.

More information about SEO can be found by google searching '*free SEO*' and then read up on what you find.

Having created your site with SEO in mind, you will then need a 'domain name' and a 'host' in order to go on line. A typical *.com* or *.co.uk* domain name costs £5 - £10 per year and can be obtained from http://www.123-reg.co.uk/ or http://heartinternet.co.uk (both good).

Then you will need your 'host'. You will have to transfer the name server to the host via the control panel in 123-reg or heartinternet to your chosen host - honestly it's not as complicated as it sounds, - or maybe it's just because I haven't got any hair left to pull out!

Beware of sites offering you a *free* domain name if you use their hosting, as there will inevitably be a *sting in the tail* and you will eventually have to pay for the name (and more) when you leave them to get hosting elsewhere. **Always buy your domain name** and retain ownership of same!

Many hosts offer you an initial low cost incentive and then screw you later in the hope that you can't cope with all the grief of changing.

If you are on a tight budget, to begin with you could use a free host such as http://000webhost.com which is also free of annoying adverts unlike most of the free hosts, but I have to say that this is not the perfect solution - just possibly a budget option to get you going.

I personally use a paid hosting, which enables me to host all my domains for one annual charge (about £40 per year) and I have to say this is far more reliable than the free option. And furthermore this allows me to keep complete control of my websites without getting ripped off as well as access to valuable help and assistance when necessary!

Should you have a brochure, price list or menu etc., you can make these into pdf files (via MS word or other software) and easily add these to your site as instant downloads. The eBook version of this book for instance is a pdf download from my site and was originally created in MS word.

So all in all a website should cost you very little and will help generate both business and profile.

## Google Adwords

Google Adwords is a method whereby you can create online adverts for your website and pay on a *per click* basis. You choose how much you are prepared to pay *per click* and this could be anything from a single penny to £5.00 or more. The more you pay, the more exposure you will get - but it won't necessarily bring you orders.

Whether this method will be any good for you will obviously depend on your type of business. I'll be honest - I can't make it worthwhile, but clearly it works for some people. It could be that I'm doing it wrong! At the time of writing this I'm still trying.

But be warned if you set this up and forget about it without *pausing* all your adverts, you could end up with a very nasty unexpected bill!

See: http://www.google.co.uk/adwords for more information.

## Video

Make a free You Tube video! This can be done easily via 'windows movie maker' with a combination of text and photos/graphics which you can zoom in and out to create the illusion of movement, or of course if you are able to, you can make a 'proper' video.

This can then be incorporated into your website (and other sites) which could increase your profile and search ratings.

I have a few videos in my sites, to be honest the early ones aren't very good, but when I get round to it I'll improve them as I'm getting better at it all the time.

Look at http://www.learn-keyboard.co.uk/lullaby_video.html and http://www.deep-relaxation.co.uk/tibetan_bells_video.html for a couple of examples of mine. And remember these cost nothing to make and nothing to put onto You Tube.

## Online Auction Sites

When you think of online auctions, unless you've been asleep for the last 10 years you would automatically think 'ebay'. But there are others, although with ebay being so strong most fail, but 'ebid' and 'bonanza' are holding their own and will get better if just more people used them. I hope that they survive and prosper as the ebay *monopoly* is not good.

Probably the most up and coming internet selling site is 'Gumtree', and guess who owns them - ebay! So they are clearly set to get bigger and remember it costs nothing to advertise your goods/services with them *and* hyperlink to your video (and website for a fee).

Anyway ebay or similar can be a superb media depending on what you are selling. The clear advantage of course is that you have worldwide coverage for a very low cost and it is also basically safe unless you do anything really stupid. The downside is that everyone wants everything for nothing on ebay so always set a starting price or a reserve.

Another disadvantage is that if you inadvertently infringe one of their many hugely ambiguous rules (or even if they think you might have); they could suspend you without warning. And as communicating with them is like trying to swing a pendulum in a bucket of glue, I would advise against building a business that relies on them more than 50% - remember: don't put all your eggs in one basket - especially that one!

## Yellow Pages

If you intend operating a local business (as against mail order etc.) then having an entry in the Yellow Pages is essential and thoroughly worthwhile. However, I know for a fact that a huge advert doesn't do much better than a small semi display type (which is what I used to use with the driving school). When potential clients/customers are looking through the Yellow pages, they will look at all the adverts large and small, but remember the right hand page rule - this still applies.

Some people have told me in the past that they are actually put off by large adverts as they think that their goods/services are going to be most expensive - and they're usually right!

You'll no doubt be aware that it can take up to a year before any benefits from the Yellow Pages kick in due to the fact that they are published annually.

**Word of Mouth recommendations**

Whatever business/occupation you're involved in, you will have a far greater chance of success if you treat your customers/clients with:

- Respect;
- Honesty;
- Efficiency;
- Reliability; and
- Offer good value for money.

If you run a small local business, personal recommendations will literally make you or break you, and without doubt is the most powerful form of all advertising, even though it basically costs you nothing.

In every business that I've run, I've made every effort to comply with the above, which is why I managed to expand my driving school to one of the largest private schools in South Yorkshire. I didn't just get recommended because of first time passes, I've had clients fail the test repeatedly and still come back and *still* recommend me.

And you may notice that with my current dealings through ebay I have acquired well over 1000 'brownie points' and a 100% positive rating.

But remember that personal recommendations work both ways. If you prove to be dishonest, unreliable or give a bad service, the word will get around to your detriment!

**Leaflets/Posters**

The cost of designing, printing and delivering leaflets can make this method non cost effective unless you sell a product/service that is potentially required by every house that they're delivered to - like hairdressing, patio cleaning or hedge trimming for instance.

When establishing the driving school I used this method despite the fact that the business did not really fit into the above criteria. To keep costs down I designed, printed and delivered all the leaflets myself, which I can tell you was hard work. The results weren't brilliant, although *it did work* to a certain extent, but was not really suitable for driving schools.

**Shop Window Adverts**

It might not seem very *hi tech*, but shop window adverts can be very effective for small local businesses. And the low cost means that you can *blitz* an area very cheaply.

Good quality coloured adverts can easily be produced using any computer/printer. Laminating will extend their life and prevent condensation damage.

Also watch prices as these can vary considerably from nothing to £1 per week. Getting these onto workplace notice boards can often be done for free. I've gained an enormous amount of business this way, particularly via nurse's residences notice boards (offering them a discount).

**Discounts, Special Offers & Freebies**

Everyone loves a freebie, even if they have to pay for it! Recently in our local supermarket there were two offers on PG tea; 240 for £2.49 and 160 for £4.25 with a free monkey. So which one did I buy? I bought both - one because it was a good deal and the other because I wanted a *free* monkey, even though it cost me over £2.50. But I do have the right to be stupid sometimes!

You'll notice that all the large pub/restaurant chains have offers on at off peak days, times and months. These give good value to the punters and gets *bums on seats* for the businesses.

There's a restaurant in Sheffield and Lincoln called Damon's who offer a free meal to everyone on their birthday (regardless of the cost of the meal). Of course they assume that others in the party will be eating as well and paying. What a brilliant concept! Every day is someone's birthday, so the place is packed every day! And you can guarantee that half the people there were born the same day as you!

Obviously the offer is geared into the prices and if a couple were born on the same day and went together they (Damon's) probably wouldn't be too happy, but I asked them about this (on my birthday) and they said that they *would* honour it.

Offers that you could make include:

- Discounts for nurses, unemployed, OAP's, students etc. (at selected times);
- Free Gifts, but remember anything that you give away affects your GP unless you give something useful that has cost you nothing;
- Discounts for multiple purchases etc.

Of course all these can and should be incorporated into most of the advertising media already mentioned.

**Advertising Gifts**

Advertising gifts with your name, phone number and web details can be very effective, but think about it from the client's point of view. Are they going to keep it or chuck it straight in the bin? Cheap pens are a complete waste of money. Affective items include:

- Key Fobs (acrylic or leather);
- Fridge magnets/magnetic business cards;
- Calendars;
- Mouse mats;
- Coasters;
- Expensive Pens;
- Descent looking paper weights.

**Exhibitions/Trade Fairs**

Exhibitions and trade fairs can be an excellent way of promoting your business and/or even generating sales on the day. But you must weigh up the cost of the pitch/stall in relation to the good it may do. Some are prohibitively expensive.

When I had the driving school supplies business there was a three day annual event at Silverstone racecourse for driving schools exclusively. I regularly had a small pitch at this event. Even over 20 years ago this cost about £250 for the 3 days, plus the cost of a hotel, but it was well worth it. Due to the nature of the event and the items I was supplying, it was a perfect match.

But despite this, I still made sure that I had plenty of low cost items (magnetic stickers etc.), that everyone felt happy about parting with their cash for (big point remember this), as well as taking many orders for larger items like roof signs etc.

I and my wife were so busy that we hardly had time to get a cup of tea but went home with a few thousand pounds in cash (mainly coins).

Due to the nature of my business there were few similar opportunities, but there may well be for other businesses.

Buying tailor made display units for exhibitions will of course improve your profile, but not necessarily your profits, so only buy them if you intend them to be used regularly. I only ever used a large table, but fortunately was selling stuff that everyone wanted to buy.

## Stationery

Very often the first thing potential new business owners do is order a 'starter pack' of useless stationery before even considering a business logo/profile etc., or what they actually need. Having been involved in printing I've always found this amusing.

It was astonishing how many letter headings and compliment slips I sold to new driving schools. Yet with my driving school, during a 30 year period I don't think I needed more than 10 letterheads and I can't remember ever using a compliment slip. So think carefully what you actually need. But of course most businesses will need business cards which are available in a huge variety of qualities and prices.

In most cases the items that you only use occasionally can be produced easily and economically on your computer/printer. If you need to produce average quantities of black printed items it might be worth your while buying a mono laser printer which can produce top quality results at a fraction of the 'ink costs' of the ink jet printers. Even *colour* laser printers are now economically available.

Depending on your type of business, you may need to issue numbered invoices and keep copies for your records (tax & VAT). But even these can be computer generated rather than professionally printed.

**Company Logo/Profile**

Most mega organizations choose logos that are basically simple and usually only two or three colours max, which can then be reproduced easily and effectively in virtually any printing/sign making medium.

It's generally the very small businesses that tend to use complicated multicoloured logos that can only be reproduced by photographic (expensive) means. Think about it!

Should you decide to have a logo; it can be anything you want with or without a particular meaning. Or you can just use a particular type face as do Sainsbury's and Tesco's.

Take a look at the website: http://www.brandsoftheworld.com. You'll be amazed at how simple many are and it could also give you some ideas. Ironically, most of these companies probably paid some 'genius' thousands of pounds for the designs.

I've absolutely no respect for British Gas at all due to the way they've treat me in the past, but I love their logo, it's so simple, yet so effective!

*British Gas*

Just think for a moment what MacDonald's would be like if it was stripped of its profile! Take all the hype away and what's left? - A burger that doesn't look anywhere near as good as the photo!

And what's Subway without its profile? - A sandwich shop! Anyone can make a sandwich! But both these companies charge huge sums for their franchises - basically for the profile! Don't get me wrong, I'm not knocking them - quite the contrary. But anyone could do it!

One day someone will come up with the idea of making square burgers and make a fortune, or burgers with holes in the middle that fit into bagels - bagelburger.com? - remember you saw this first here! Do it - someone will - and I'm not bothered! But don't worry if you 'miss the boat'; there's always triangles and pentagons etc!

Anything and everything can be made:

- Bigger or Smaller;
- Faster or Slower;
- A different shape or colour;
- Softer or Harder etc., etc.

There is no end to creative thought!

## Xmas/Birthday Cards

Keeping birthday records of clients/potential clients can be worthwhile, enabling you to send them a card to remember you! As with many stationery items, personalized cards can easily be made on your computer (in A4 size then fold into four). But remember that Jews, Muslims and some other religions don't celebrate Christmas, but most celebrate birthdays and New Year.

And of course we now have 'e-cards', but personally I think they're a bit naff - but I am getting ancient!

## Social Media

There's no doubt about it that Facebook and the like are a formidable force and can be geared to increase your business.

But I have to say that building a truly effective network could be very time consuming. I personally don't like Facebook, and find the idea of being 'followed' on twitter positively creepy!

Linkedin seems more sensible to me for business users and you are certainly welcome to link to my network if you wish.

But whatever you think about these, it's a good idea to add all their 'like' icons to your website in the hope that someone might 'like' you!

# Selling Your Business

It's surprising how many sole traders never actually cash in on all the hard work that they've put into building their businesses. It takes time, effort and money to establish a business and this should be recognized in the sale value. But sadly many just fold up and retire.

Remember, I'm and old git and have done the full cycle: *starting, running and selling* several times.

Ok, so how much is a business worth? Some are very difficult to put a price to, but the value consists of:

- Property or lease value;
- Fixtures, fittings and machinery etc.;
- Goodwill/client base;
- Stock at valuation (where necessary).

Clearly the goodwill is the difficult part to value and is based on:

- Length of time the business has been established;
- Client base;
- Annual turnover and net profit supported by at least 3 years certified accounts or verified income tax computations.

When considering selling, bear in mind that it may take quite some time to find a suitable buyer, so go on the market early and try to avoid putting yourself in a position where you are desperate to sell. Every town and city has agents who specialise in business sales and many more can be found in the Daltons Weekly: http://www.daltons.co.uk. You will undoubtedly find similar outside of the UK.

I've sold all of my businesses, but only one through an agent (the driving school supplies). The driving school was sold to one of my instructors who waited a year until I was ready to sell, and my sign business in Cyprus was sold privately out there the day before we left (by prior arrangement).

When selling it's normal to have a signed agreement with the buyer stating that you will not start up a similar business within a certain distance and/or time scale which of course is reasonable and fair. But there's normally nothing to stop you starting up in another town or do what Nemo does, operate a different business for a few years.

Finally remember that the profit from the sale of the business could be liable for capital gains tax. The rules on this are forever changing so seek professional advice. But if your business is jointly owned with your wife or partner, then you can both take advantage of the capital gains tax allowances.

# Tax & VAT

Please note that as there many are Tax variations worldwide which change on an annual basis, this information should only be taken as a *rough* guide. Obviously professional up to date local information should be sought as and when required. The information here is applicable to the UK at the time of the latest update (2013).

Keeping detailed and accurate accounts of your trading figures is not only essential and a legal requirement from the Income Tax and VAT (if applicable) point of view, but it's also your only way of keeping a check on your progress and thereby maximizing your *net* profits.

## Income Tax & Accounts Preparation

There are many simple accounts programs on the market specifically designed for small businesses, or you could create your own using MS excel as I do. But whatever you decide the important thing is to get into the habit or imputing your entries on a daily basis at the same time as numbering and filing you receipts/invoices. This will avert a crisis at the end of the year.

Whether you are VAT registered or not always get VAT receipts for all your expenditure. Acquire a ring binder to save all your receipts in a numbered order, coinciding with numbering in your accounts system so that any receipt can be identified and located easily. If receipts are too small, attach them to a larger piece of paper to fit in the binder.

If due to the nature of your business, you issue invoices, then copies of these should be kept and filed the same way in another binder. The Inland Revenue requires that you keep all receipts, invoices and bank statements for a period of six years.

Where a particular expense is only partially for business use (telephone/vehicle etc.) then you will only be able to claim tax relief for the business proportion, but this can be ignored in the initial accounts and adjusted in the summary.

Whatever software you use, it will probably have the main categories and sub categories for income and expenditure already listed, but will allow you to edit these and add more as required. It should also allow you to view and print out a full summary at any time, which you can use at the end of the year to help complete your self assessment income tax form. Although initially, you are advised to let your accountant take care of this for you. But if you keep records and receipts clearly entered and filed as suggested on a regular basis, you will save yourself a nightmare and reduce you accountant's bill.

Your end of year summary will look something like this:

| | |
|---|---|
| Total Income | £75,000.00 |
| Cost of Sales | £10,000.00 |
| **Gross Profit** | **£65,000.00** |
| | |
| **Expenses:** | |
| Wages to Wife | £8,000.00 |
| Advertising | £15,000.00 |
| Motoring | £12,000.00 |
| Telephone/Internet | £600.00 |
| Utilities | £1,800.00 |
| Printing/Stationery | £600.00 |
| Interest on loans | £500.00 |
| Legal/Professional | £500.00 |
| **Total Expenses** | **£39,000.00** |
| | |
| **Net Profit** | **£26,000.00** |

Of course your figures may not be anything like these, but the format should be similar. Income tax will become payable on the net profit less your personal tax allowance and less any capital allowances which we'll deal with now.

**Capital Allowances**

Items such as computers, motor vehicles, tools, machinery, office equipment etc., are capital expenditure and each year a capital allowance can be claimed against these, which is continued in successive years until the item(s) is either sold or written off when a balancing charge or allowance is levied to balance things out.

For instance if you bought a car for £10,000 the computation would be as follows:

### Capital Allowance Year 1

| | |
|---|---|
| Purchase Price | £10,000.00 |
| Capital Allowance 18% | £1,800.00 |
| **Writing Down Value** | **£8,200.00** |

### Capital Allowance Year 2

| | |
|---|---|
| Writing Down Value b/f | £8,200.00 |
| Capital Allowance 18% | £1,476.00 |
| **Writing Down Value** | **£6,724.00** |

### Capital Allowance Year 3

| | |
|---|---|
| Writing Down Value b/f | £6,724.00 |
| Sale Price | £7,200.00 |
| **Balancing Charge** | **-£476.00** |

### Year 3 (alternative)

| | |
|---|---|
| Writing Down Value b/f | £6,724.00 |
| Sale Price | £5,000.00 |
| **Balancing Allowance** | **£1,724.00** |

This incidentally doesn't mean that you would pay the £476 balancing charge, but it would be the same as though this amount was added to your net profit, or deducted from your expenses - it would be taxable.

In all cases if the item was used only partially for business use, then only the relevant proportion can be claimed (or re-claimed in the event of a balancing allowance).

## Income Tax Computations

Following are a couple of typical tax computation examples:

### Income Tax Computation

| | |
|---|---|
| Net Profit | £26,000.00 less |
| Personal Allowance | £8,105.00 |
| Capital Allowances | £1,800.00 |
| Taxable Income | £16,095.00 |
| | |
| **Tax Payable @ 20%** | **£3,219.00** |

### Income Tax Computation

| | |
|---|---|
| Net Profit | £26,000.00 less |
| Personal Allowance | £8,105.00 |
| Capital Allowances | - |
| Balancing Charge | -£476.00 |
| Taxable Income | £18,371.00 |
| | |
| **Tax Payable @ 20%** | **£3,674.20** |

## Paying your Tax

Self employment tax in the UK is payable in two equal instalments on 31st January and 31st July of each year. So when you first start in business, in your first year of trading your tax bill will be delayed (but not forgotten) until after your first years self assessment form has been completed. Then you will be required to pay for the first year *plus* the same amount again (with the January payment) in advance for the next year which is then adjusted up or down after the next self assessment form has been submitted.

So make sure from day one that you save at least 20% of your net profit in readiness for this payment. Remember this is not your money and the Inland Revenue will pursue you ruthlessly for this - so be prepared.

So to make this clearer, if you started in business in April 2010 you would complete your first self assessment form in April 2011 and would receive your first tax bill for payment in January 2012 for the 2010/11 year (in full) *plus* the first instalment for the year 2011/12 and the second instalment in July. This will obviously make the first (January 2012) payment very high and a very nasty shock if you're not prepared for it. And this is certainly one of the reasons that 2/3rds of new businesses go bust in the first year - bad accounting and spending money that's not theirs! You've been warned! - Ignore this at your peril!

**Tax Enquires**

The UK income tax self assessment system relies on the fact that everyone enters the correct figures on their return forms and thereby pays the correct amount of tax.

To reduce mistakes and fraud, it's normal for the Inland Revenue to occasionally take a closer look. This could be anything from a simple enquiry about certain items on your tax form, to a full scale 'enquiry' where you would be required to attend the tax offices with all your detailed accounts, receipts and bank statements etc.

This is particularly likely to occur if your accounts suggest that something is incorrect, like you are covering 200,000 miles a year in a Smart car that is only doing 5 mpg etc. Most abnormalities stick out like a sore thumb!

If you operate a 'cash' business, the Inland Revenue may also want to see evidence of your personal expenditure and if this happens to be more than your net income - you're in trouble. So be prepared!

Just before we left for Cyprus in 2003 I underwent one of these 'enquiries' which lasted from February until September, during which time I was constantly wandering around in a daze with a calculator trying to figure out how much they were going to 'screw' me.

The end result was nowhere near as bad as imagined and ended up costing me less than £300, as it was found that I'd apparently failed to disclose some credit card 'points' which I'd saved and used as part payment for a business car. And our pet poodle was disallowed as a guard dog despite the fact that he was more mentally deranged than the average rabid Alsatian!

A tax 'investigation' incidentally is far more invasive than an 'enquiry'. I dread to think what one of these entails!

## Capital Gains Tax

Other than the house that you may own and occupy, you could be required to pay capital gains tax on the profits from any asset sold if either of the following apply:

- Your chargeable gains - before deducting any losses - are more than the Annual Exempt Amount - £10,600 in 2012-13;

- The total amount you received from selling or disposing of assets is more than £42,400 in 2012-13.

As a self employed person this will normally affect you when selling:

- Your Business;
- Business Premises;
- Buy to Let Properties;
- Stocks and Shares.

In addition to your personal tax allowance of £8,105, which will no doubt be used up with your 'normal' income, everyone has a capital gains tax allowance of £10,600, and then taxable gains are (currently) charged at a flat rate of 18% on the lower rate of tax increasing to 28% for the higher rate.

Bearing in mind that you may have owned the property for 15 - 20 years or more remember that from day one it's important to prepare for the final selling day by:

- Keeping receipts relating to buying/selling costs;
- Keeping receipts for building improvements etc. (which must not have been claimed previously as revenue expenses);
- Keep records of any mortgage redemption fees.

A typical Capital Gains Tax example is as follows:

### Capital Gains Tax

| | |
|---|---|
| Property Purchase Price | £50,000.00 |
| Property Selling Price | £120,000.00 |
| Gross Gain | £70,000.00 |

| | |
|---|---|
| Buying/Selling Fees | £5,000.00 |
| Property Improvements | £20,000.00 |
| Mortgage Redemption Fees | £2,000.00 |
| Total Expenses | £27,000.00 |
| | |
| Net Gain | £43,000.00 |
| Less Personal Allowance | 10,600.00 |
| Taxable Gain | £32,400.00 |
| | |
| **Tax Payable @ 18%** | **£5,832.00** |

Note that if the property was/is purchased in joint names by you and your partner then you would both benefit from the capital gains tax allowance and the tax liability would then reduce by £1,908 (£10,600 @18%).

The same applies to buying/selling the business - joint ownership can be an advantage. And in the case of selling your business, you may be eligible for the entrepreneur's allowance which could reduce your liability to 10% instead of 18%, but remember that these rules are forever changing, so this may or may not apply to you when you sell your business.

Going back to the example of Nemo's success, notice that when he sold his businesses he retained the property and thereby reduced his capital gains tax liability. No doubt when he eventually sells these he will do so in different tax years thereby maximizing his capital gains tax allowances. And being shrewd he will almost certainly have the businesses and properties in joint names with his wife.

Avoiding capital gains tax on stocks and shares is easy. Simply sell shares with a gain not exceeding the value of your allowance at the end of the UK financial year (April 5th) and then buy them back again at the beginning of the next financial year (April 6th) if you so wish.

But before disposing of anything that may incur capital gains tax, be sure to consult your accountant as he's bound to know the best way to minimize the liability.

## VAT

Any (UK) business with a turnover approaching or in excess of £79,000 (2013) is required to register for VAT. Businesses with lower turnovers may also register if they wish. However in most cases there are no benefits in registering as in effect you would become an unpaid tax collector and be forced to increase your prices/fees by 20% or take the loss yourself - a loss that could destroy you!

There are only two possible exceptions:

- If you are selling a zero rated item (like milk or nappies), in this case you would actually receive a VAT refund on your *vatable* expenses;

- If you deal exclusively with other VAT registered businesses, who could reclaim the VAT that you charge.

Apart from these two exceptions I would avoid registering, and having been a member of this nasty little club, I would make sure that my turnover never reached the required level again at any costs.

Note that fuel is not necessarily an eligible expense, different rules apply and in many cases it's just not worth claiming for this.

And it's quite possible to earn a good living without your turnover reaching £79,000. Dealing in stocks and shares or property is exempt from VAT (apart from certain fees).

Another possible way to avoid registering is by splitting your business into two (one yours and one your partners), and in this event the accounts must be *completely* separate - but consult your accountant for more details of whether this could be possible in your circumstances. And of course if you did this you wouldn't be able to take advantage of the capital gains tax reduction as previously mentioned above by having your business in joint names.

But if you do have to or wish to register for VAT, this is payable quarterly and a typical example is as follows:

### Quarterly VAT Return

|  | Inc. Vat | Vat 20% |
|---|---|---|
| Turnover (3 months) | £16,500.00 | £2,750.00 |
| Eligible Expenses | £3,500.00 | £583.33 |
| **VAT Payable for quarter** | | **£2,166.67** |

If you think about it, you will see that if you weren't registered this amount would be reduced to **£583.33**, (the VAT in the expenses that you wouldn't be able to reclaim).

In addition to preparing the VAT accounts, all the invoices and receipts need to be collated and numbered as previously suggested. And you will also have periodic visits from the VAT inspectors.

I only ever had one of these visits - from a female VAT inspector. Had she been Hitler's daughter, he would have been extremely proud of her!

# Pensions

If you have any existing private or company pensions, it's probably best to leave them as they are. But if you are considering buying a new private pension, think very carefully as few people really understand the full implications. Here are a few points to consider:

- Any money that you pay into a private pension becomes out of your control until you're 60 years old and even then you can only get your paws on 25% of it, as the rest must be used to buy an annuity or re-invested in a way that only allows you to take an income;

- Most pension companies don't even outperform the stock market, yet charge you an annual percentage for their gross inefficiency;

- Some companies charges are outrageous and often hidden, particularly when you pay a lump sum in one year;

- Yes there are tax advantages to private pensions, but you need to decide whether this advantage is worth the loss of control and their fees - I decided not.

Just in case you don't know, an annuity is an agreement where you hand over your pension pot (or any other sum of money) in exchange for a monthly pension for the rest of your life, but these are rarely index linked, so in real terms will erode in value as time passes. The amount of income you receive is agreed at the time of purchase (which depends on your age and health etc.) and then remains unchanged for the duration. But what a particular sum would buy you can vary from month to month depending on the state of the stock market and interest rates. At the time of writing this, annuity payouts are very low, less than half of what they were a few years ago.

And of course remember that if you snuff it six months after taking out the annuity, they win big time, not that you'd be particularly bothered but your poor grieving off springs (and spouse unless you have joint annuities) would lose out badly.

An alternative to a pension fund is simply to make your own investments, and then you will be in complete control and if you did nothing more than track the stock market, you'd probably do better than a pension fund and wouldn't have to pay their fees. The downside is that you would lose the tax benefits, but you need to weigh this up against the fees and loss of control. For me there's no contest and of course you could still buy an annuity at any time if you so wished.

Even buying Gold Krugerrands, one at a time as you can afford them would probably beat the Stock Market when you take into account the fees. And most importantly you would retain control of your assets. There's also something 'real' and comforting about holding a gold coin compared to looking at figure on a bank statement.

Buying gold (or any other investment) on a monthly basis means that you would buy at the market *highs* and the *lows* and this usually averages out quite favourably.

Another thing you could do to secure your pension with complete control is to buy property for rental/investment and with property prices being so low right now, there's actually never been a better time. And if you do it right, it can be virtually self financing!

See my guides: 'Buy to Let on a Budget', 'An Introduction to Traded Options' and 'The Richest Man in Babylon' (the free link for this last item is included with your bonus items).

---

### DISCLAIMER

Every effort has been made to ensure that the information herein is correct, but as laws and regulations are constantly changing, no responsibility can be accepted for any inaccuracies.

You are therefore advised to seek independent and professional advice before acting on any of the advice contained herein.

# Your Belief Zone and More!

The information given so far is good, honest, workable advice that should enable anyone to begin working for themselves profitably to either a small or large degree.

But if you've never been in business before, you will probably find a big stumbling block in the fact that you might not *believe* that you can do it - this is what I call your **'Belief Zone!'**

Now if you've never heard of anything like this before you may think that what follows is a complete load of cobblers, but I can assure you that every successful business person uses the information that follows (either consciously or subconsciously) and furthermore every unsuccessful person also uses it - but incorrectly. It's a Universal law that absolutely has to happen. So there's no question as to whether you can do it or not - you already are!

**"There is a thinking stuff from which all things are made, and which, in its original state permeates, penetrates and fills the interspaces of the universe.**

**A thought, in this substance, produces the thing that is imaged by the thought.**

**Man can form things in his thought, and, by impressing his thought upon formless substance, can cause the thing he thinks about to be created."** - Wallace Wattles - The Science of Getting Rich.

## Your Belief Zone

If all the wealth in the world was gathered up and shared out equally among the world's population, I'd like to bet that within five years it would all be back where it is now. And this is because we all have a self inflicted *'belief zone'* which is very difficult to break out of. This is the reason that most 'get rich quick' schemes don't work. Actually some of them can work, but not if they take you out of your belief zone!

As an example, when I first started as a driving instructor, I worked for someone else for a short while, because I didn't believe that I could generate any business on my own. Then, after not very long I thought -

'Stuff this - I don't need him, I can do this on my own!' So I did, and very successfully. In fact without me being consciously aware of it my belief zone expanded slightly allowing this to happen.

Then as my business expanded, the instructors who worked for me (many whom I trained) had the same problem - they believed that they would be successful if they worked for me. And curiously even though I did nothing different, the work for each new instructor just happened. You may not believe this but I know that it was *their* belief, coupled with mine that made this happen - the belief that they would get work with me but not on their own! This happened numerous times enabling my school to expand - but of course I worked hard at it as well. Then as each instructor's belief zone expanded, they too left me to go their own way and I never discouraged this. But as they left, more came to take their place and I carried on expanding - such was *my* belief!

This belief zone works at all levels and is the reason that big businesses get and remain big - but remember it's not just the belief of the directors/owners, it's also the belief of the workers, and the power is formidable!

Of course some people develop a big belief zone in early childhood due to parental and environmental circumstances while others apparently are less fortunate, but the power is the same - you will get what you believe!

And if your belief zone is lousy - fear not - it can be fixed!

**Improving Your Belief Zone**

Over the years there's been many inspirational books written on this subject. In my opinion some of the best of these are:

- Think and Grow Rich - Napoleon Hill*

- The Science of Getting Rich - Wallace Wattles*

- The Magic of Thinking Big - David J Schwartz

- The Magic of Believing - Claude M Bristol*

- The Lazy Man's Way to Riches - Joe Karbo

- The Secret - Rhonda Byrne*

The ones marked with the * are all available as Free downloads as most are now in the public domain. Details of where to obtain all of these free links will be given further on.

You would be wise to download and digest all of these, but basically I have to say that they all give the same message but of course with their own individual 'twist'. I suggest that you read The Science of Getting Rich first (at least 5 times if you're serious) and don't be put off by the fact that it was written over 100 years ago and speaks of commercial air travel and electric trains as possible future events! - The message is as relevant today as it ever was!

Having read all of them and others I shall herewith summarise that basic message with all the waffle removed.

## The Vast Power of Your Mind

You have the power to turn the sea into custard if you really want to and really believe that you can. But fortunately you probably don't believe that you can and probably don't want to anyway, so all the fish can sleep soundly *in their beds* at night!

## An Experiment

Obtain a large variety of different seeds - some flowers - some vegetables, put them all into a large bowl and mix them all up. Then add some dandelion and some other 'weedy' seeds and for good measure chuck in some ivy. Next, plant them all together anywhere. Don't worry about the soil - just chuck them in. If you want to you can water them a bit to get them going or just neglect them and let nature take its course - it makes no difference.

What do you think you would end up with? Well you would most certainly get a result - a chaotic mess - 100% of what you asked for! Amazingly some of the good stuff would survive, but of course much of it would be killed off by the weeds.

Now think of how things would have been different if you had not mixed up all the seeds, but had chosen which to plant and had taken just a little care about the soil quality, watered them when necessary and removed any weeds as they emerged.

I don't think that you really need to try this experiment to prove the results. It's obvious that 'you reap what you sow' - it's a Universal law - it must happen. But if you feel the need to prove it - do so - the choice is yours.

Now, in case you've not already figured it out, your thoughts can be compared to the seeds, your mind the flower bed, repetition the water and the result is your conscious experience.

We're all 'guilty' of jumbled uncontrolled thoughts (at least to a degree), the result of which is governed by the same Universal law. In fact it's amazing that our lives are not more chaotic than they are given the amount of 'propaganda' that's banged into us from all angles. Unless you live in a cave you can't get away from it. We are constantly told: what to eat; what to wear; how we should look; how we should act etc., etc. via billboards; TV; newspapers; friends and family etc. And 99% of it is total garbage.

Although you can't get away from the perpetual advertising and environmental influences etc. you can take steps to neutralize it. Firstly by becoming aware of it, secondly by deciding how YOU want to live and finally by 'reprogramming' yourself accordingly.

Every action is preceded by a thought (FACT). If the thought is 'right' (whatever 'right' may happen to be) then 'right' action will follow. But if you are not in control of your thoughts (which most of us aren't), you are certainly not in control of your actions.

You might think that this is all complete nonsense, but the multi million pound marketing companies know it's not and dearly hope that you never discover the truth.

Either you take conscious control of your thoughts (and actions) or someone else will. Do you want to remain a puppet or a master of your own destiny?

### The Universal Subjective/Subconscious Mind

You are in direct and constant communication with every*body* and every*thing* in existence (whether you like it or not). As well as having an individual subconscious mind, we are all connected to the same Universal Subjective mind which is why and how we (mainly unconsciously through our personal subconscious) 'influence' (but not 'control') other people/animals/elements etc. to create situations that we want (or don't want depending on how we influence them).

All your thoughts, wishes, fears and especially your 'spoken word' are reflected into the Universal Subconscious and then channelled out in different directions to bring about your conscious experience. And this is all achieved without any conscious effort of any kind.

Even every material 'thing' is a thought materialised. You can bring into being any 'thing' or 'situation' that you really want or don't want either deliberately or accidentally.

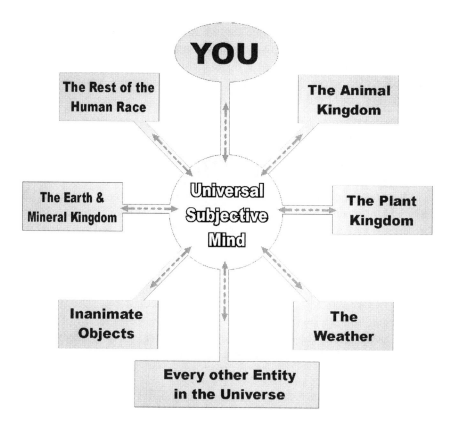

## Some Personal Experiences

Back in the 60's when I was a teenager; the only thing that I wanted to do was be a professional 'pop' musician. The only exams I passed at school were music. Nothing else mattered to me.

After leaving school, I worked in a music publishers for a while, playing gigs in the evenings. But it wasn't long before I was a professional musician as I wanted so much.

But then I wanted/needed a Hammond organ. At the time these cost about £2,000. To put this in perspective a house in South London cost about £5,000. So clearly relatively speaking they were incredibly expensive and my chance of affording one was about nil.

Nevertheless I was in all of the London music shops virtually on a daily basis 'trying them out'. I never actually got slung out, but they must have been sick to death of me! My bedside cupboard was full of Hammond colour brochures which I used to study in detail before falling asleep to dream about them.

In my mind I could feel my fingers on the keys, smell the veneer, hear the various tones and picture the various models in extreme detail. I used to imagine playing one on stage in front of huge screaming audiences. However I must state that I was never very good at 'visualising', but I did 'imagine' it clearly.

Actually without knowing it I was using a very powerful technique very effectively (albeit in a slightly unrefined way) and I was doing it 'passionately' - with much emotion. And guess what happened - I ended up owning the Hammond of my dreams!

Of course the multinational advertising giants are well aware of all this which is why they spend a small fortune producing the glossy brochures and why they encourage you to test drive that new car, or organ, or whatever.

Anyway, over the next few years I also ended playing keyboards with some of my favourite bands - Geno Washington and the Ramjam Band; The Fantastics; Emile Ford and the Checkmates; The Tommy Hunt Band and my own band 'Aquila'. If you've never heard of any of these - sadly I have to say 'Ask your grandmother' - who probably has! Had I been aware of the information I now have, I would have achieved far better results.

After achieving my dreams and spending a few years 'on the road' touring everywhere and playing to 'huge screaming audiences', doing TV and recording work, I then realised that although I loved the music I didn't really like the lifestyle very much. I've never been much of a 'party goer' but I was living in a party 24/7. So partly very reluctantly I gave up touring, which actually was almost as difficult as getting into it in the first place. Finding conventional employment when all I knew was music was not easy.

Anyway driving tuition became my game and it wasn't long before I was the proprietor of one of Sheffield's largest and most successful schools. However by this time I was far more aware of the techniques outlined here and used them to build my business.

Using these same techniques I also started a successful mail order sign business (as well as running the driving school) and got into 'buy to let' properties. I used the same techniques to sell all of these businesses and retire to Cyprus aged 54, where we had a lovely villa with a pool overlooking the sea.

This sounds idyllic doesn't it? But it's not exactly what it seems. In fact there's many ex pats out there literally drinking themselves to death through boredom. And the heat in July and August is unbelievable - what you save in heating bills you spend on air-conditioning. And having a swimming pool I found more of a burden and no big deal. But having said all this I'm very glad that I did it, so that at least I can move on.

In 2006 after 3 years of *'living the dream'* in Cyprus we decided to return to the UK due to the unbearable summer heat. In the January of 2006 I booked fixed date flights for us to return to the UK at the beginning of August, and then (in January) we put our villa on the market as well as the sign business that I had started out there. At that time property was simply not selling. Even though our villa had all the trimmings, there were literally hundreds of lovely villas just as good as ours also on the market and not selling.

Anyway to cut a long story short, we sold the villa for the asking price to a cash buyer (from a private advert in the local paper) and also the sign business to a different buyer and our car (to someone else) all within four days of the flight which I'd booked 6 months previously. Coincidence? - I *know* it wasn't, but you can think what you like!


**Your Word is Power**

Every word that we hear, speak or think has some power. Listening to, speaking or even thinking apparently innocent statements such as the following over a period of time could affect you accordingly (for 'good' or for 'bad'):

- My feet are 'killing' me;
- I'm 'starving/freezing' to death etc.;
- It 'always rains' when I have a day off;
- I'll 'never win' the lottery/be rich/pass the driving test etc.;
- However much I diet 'I still can't' lose weight;
- As soon as one bill is paid I get another;
- I 'never have enough' money;
- I'm 'always broke';
- My boss always picks on me;
- However much I try, 'I can never get straight';
- I 'always get nervous' at interviews;

- I'm 'too old' to: learn to drive/go to Australia/learn music etc., etc.;
- This country is getting worse each year;
- Everything is always going up in price;
- I'm sick with worry;
- Nothing is as good as it used to be etc., etc.

Be extremely careful about what you say and think, as ultimately you will get 100% of what you ask for! - Remember the 'Three Wise Monkeys'!

IF YOU DON'T WANT 'IT' - DON'T SAY 'IT', DON'T SEE 'IT', DON'T HEAR 'IT' AND DON'T EVEN THINK 'IT'!

Spend a little while noticing how much of this rot you hear from friends/family etc. and also how much 'garbage' you tell yourself through your 'inner chatter'. The first step is being aware of it. You will eventually learn how to control it.

Not happy with what you've got? Learn to ask for something different!

**Choose Exactly What You Want**

One of the reasons that most people live in a permanent state of chaos is because they have never clearly defined exactly what it is that they want and are therefore sending out mixed messages to the 'Universal Mind' which is always happy to give you exactly what you ask for.

So now I want you to make three lists as follows:

- Material desires;
- Situations that you'd like to change;
- Personal qualities that you'd like to alter.

You can split the first two lists into short and long term goals, but the third needs only one.

| Material Examples | |
| --- | --- |
| Short Term | Long Term |
| New car | Sports car - Rolls Royce |
| New kitchen | Luxury home in the sun |
| Holiday | Luxury motorhome / yaght |
| New camera / laptop | World cruise |
| New keyboard / guitar | Total financial independence |

| Situation Examples | |
| --- | --- |
| Short Term | Long Term |
| New Job | Business of your own |
| Promotion | Be world class footballer |
| Pass driving test | Be world class musician |
| Learn to fly plane | Find ideal partner |
| Cope with illness | Cure illness |

| Personal Quailities Examples | |
| --- | --- |
| Happiness | Creativity |
| Self confidence | Increased energy |
| Ideal wieght | Increased feelings of prosperity |
| Cure addiction | Intuition |
| Soul travel | Wisdom |
| Self Realisation | |

I've given a brief example here. But your list can be as long or short as you like. You can of course change your mind as you progress (as I clearly have done many times), but try and at least get your short term lists right and also your personal qualities.

Try and make your short term lists at least believable. For instance if you are unemployed, broke and homeless (I've been there!), you would probably find it hard to believe that you could be a millionaire within a few months, and if you attempted this, you would probably get disillusioned and give up.

In this case your short term list should be getting somewhere to live and getting an income. Put being a millionaire and an airline pilot in your long term list (if this is what you want).

Remember also that every material 'thing' comes with a burden i.e.:

- Cleaning it;

- Worrying about someone stealing it;

- Insuring it;

- Repairing/servicing it;

- Replacing it when it inevitably falls apart etc.

And don't get 'needs' mixed up with 'wants'. Don't misunderstand me, I'm not saying that you shouldn't want things, or it's wrong to be rich - just make sure that you understand the difference. You 'need' warmth, food and shelter, everything else is 'wants'.

And be sure that you do actually 'own' the things that you own and not that they 'own' you! Think carefully about this!

Finally make sure that none of your desires are *'competitive'* in nature. You don't need to beat anyone to get what you want. There does not have to be *winners* and *losers* - there really is enough for everyone to have and be everything that they want!

I know that most 'businesses' by nature appear to be competitive, but they don't have to be. It's all a question of your mindset. If you just do what you do and have a good honest 'value for money' policy, ensuring that your customers receive more in 'use' value than they have paid in cash, and never try to discredit or bring down others in the same (or any) profession - then you are acting *'creatively'*.

"Only when there is no competition will we all live in peace." - Lao Tzu.

### Forming effective Suggestions/Affirmations

Having completed your lists, at least you should have a clear idea of where you would like to end up and for many people this is a big step forward.

Now we're going to convert these lists into powerful suggestions/affirmations.

To do this, you must follow these guidelines:

1. They must be short, clear and unambiguous. 'I earn more money' is incorrect as 'more' is relative and basically means nothing - how much more? A penny more? 'I have all the money that I need or want' is better. 'I have a better job' again is incorrect as 'better' is a matter of opinion -

better than what? Who determines what is better? 'I am a police Chief Inspector' could perhaps be a good short term affirmation if you are already a police constable or sergeant, but would only be good as a long term one if you are currently unemployed and aspire to this.

2. They must be 100% positive. 'I am not afraid of heights' is a negative statement and should be avoided. The subconscious will pick up on 'afraid' and ignore the 'not', which could of course make the problem worse. 'I can see myself climbing ladders confidently and safely' is better.

3. They must be clearly in the present time only. 'I will be healthy, wealthy and wise' is incorrect as the subconscious will pick up on the 'will be' and conclude that you don't actually want this to occur now and as everything can only occur in the present moment - your goal will never be achieved. 'I WILL BE' is like an unplanted seed which cannot materialise - nothing more than a 'wish'! 'I AM' is like a seed correctly planted which MUST materialise. It's a Universal Law! 'I am healthy wealthy and wise' is better.

4. There should be no time or monetary limits. The subconscious only operates in the NOW. One faulty affirmation I used a few years ago was: 'I have a successful mail order business earning £250 per week' At the time £250 per week was quite an acceptable amount, but the fact that I'd 'asked' for this amount resulted in the business getting 'stuck' at that level until I realised what had happened and corrected the fault. So if you do make monetary limits, make sure they're very high. It's only a matter of time before a loaf of bread will cost £1000 or more!

## Emile Coué 1857 - 1926

Probably the most well known affirmation is the one popularised by Emile Coué - the father of auto suggestion: 'Day by day in every way I am getting better and better'.

Although this suggestion achieved some apparently remarkable results in sick individuals it is nevertheless flawed in the fact that it uses the word 'getting' (future). The fact that it is non-specific 'in every way' was deliberate in order to deal with numerous complaints.

'Here and now in every way I AM perfect as God created me' is better.

## The Law of Reversed Effort

Also attributed to Emile Coué is the 'Law of Reversed Effort' - the more you consciously try to resist anything - the more it will persist. And is the reason that all suggestions should be worded in a 'positive' form as stated previously.

Could you walk along a plank 20' (6m) long by 3' (1m) wide if it was suspended approximately 6'' (15 cm) off the ground? Of course you could - anyone could - eazzie peazzie! Now what if it was suspended across a 200' (60m) deep ravine full of hungry crocodiles? Now you probably couldn't - I know I couldn't, but why? Because in the first example you'd see no problem and just do it, whereas in the second you and me both would be 'focussed' on falling off and being eaten by crocodiles.

This is often the case with the driving test (or other exams) and why you can drive perfectly OK with your instructor, but go to pieces when the examiner gets in. If you're 'focussed' on failing - that's exactly what YOU will bring about. If you focus on your driving (the present moment) instead of passing or failing, you will increase your chances of bringing about the favoured result.

Similarly you can't hold onto the mental image of riches while thinking about poverty, or health while reading up on sickness, or success while focussed on failure etc.

And in my own case this brought about the horrifying tax 'enquiry' which I endured before leaving for Cyprus. At the back of my mind I held a fear that the Tax man would come after me - and of course he did!

Here's another short snippet that you might find incredible. Once I knew a lady driving instructor who specialised in training disabled people to drive with a specially adapted vehicle. Tragically *she* became disabled herself!

And this is why Wallace Wattles in 'The Science of Getting Rich' states that until you have completed your task (become rich), you shouldn't involve yourself in any charitable work. I know this might seem very anti Christian, but if you think about it, it's only the same advice that you get in aeroplanes about putting *your* oxygen mask on first before helping your children - you won't be much good to them lying in a heap on the floor!

The fact remains that once *you* are rich and successful you can then do far more good to those around you!

Having correctly worded your suggestions into the three categories as indicated, we are now ready to move onto the techniques for achieving your goals.

## The Technique in Practice

This simple powerful technique can be used for any of the suggestion/affirmations in any of the three lists.

How quickly it will work will depend on your present level of negativity. 20 years of wrong thinking is probably not going to be neutralized in one or two sessions - having said that - who knows? But generally, the more often you do it the quicker it will work.

Just before falling asleep and just as you wake, you are in a natural state of hypnosis. These states are called 'hypnogogic' and 'hypnopompic' and are particularly good times to use this technique, but any other time will work also.

## Step by step

1.  Make some time for yourself when you will not be disturbed for about half an hour. Turn your mobile phone off and isolate yourself in a quiet room.

2.  Choose a up to 5 of the declarations that you want to work on.

3.  Sit or lie down in a comfortable position and relax as best you can. Taking a few deep breaths will help you do this.

4.  To get yourself in the right frame of mind, think of the happiest event in your life so far. Really try and feel it as best you can. Bringing EMOTION into the equation helps tremendously.

5.  Read the chosen declarations EXACTLY as they are written, preferably out loud (but at least verbalised) with conviction. Repeat each one a few times. If you can, try and visualise the reality of what you are saying. Using a mirror and looking into your eyes will enhance the process.

6. In between each declaration, just sit and relax for a short while.

7. Finish the session with a feeling that what you have stated is true and is a reality now - even though it isn't!

8. Choose one of the declarations (that you consider most important), write it on a card, keep it with you at all times and read it (out loud or verbalised) as often as you can think of it in between sessions (preferably every hour).

That's it - simple!

Don't confuse this with 'Will Power' or 'Positive Thinking' etc.; this is far more powerful and incredibly easy. And don't think you can't do this - you've been doing it all your life. This is just a refined version - a way of planting the seeds correctly! If you think about it carefully, it's even logical! AND IT WORKS!

Note that you DO NOT NEED to be in a hypnotic state to do this - just comfortably relaxed - but conscious. Do not fall asleep. But to fall asleep just after is perfect!

My Alpha Binaural Beats mp3 that you can download for free can be used here if required. I'll explain more about this shortly, but basically it consists only of sounds and ambient music which will assist your relaxation to exactly the ideal level.

The more you repeat these statements/declarations to yourself the sooner they will be accepted by your subconscious mind and the sooner they will become a reality for you. Once the subconscious accepts a statement it will act on it whether you like it or not! Don't worry if you feel like you are lying to yourself - just do it!

The more you do it, the more you'll believe it - the stronger the belief - the sooner it will happen. Real strong 'Belief' produces miracles.

**Aid to Visualisation**

Another good thing to do is to make a scrap book containing everything on your lists. If you can get photos of any material things or even miniature copies, these will be most useful. In fact if you google search just about anything (even abstract) and click on the 'images' section you will be able to get printable images for anything that you want!

Remember how I *accidentally* got my Hammond organ:

- I had every colour brochure available;

- I studied them consciously before falling asleep;

- I wanted it desperately;

- I played them virtually on a daily basis at all the London music shops (in rotation);

- I could feel them, hear them, see them and smell them in my mind.

In-between sessions also try and become aware of your 'inner chatter' and exactly what YOU are saying to YOU! As soon as you notice any negative nonsense, put a stop to it immediately. It's very likely that your subconscious will fight back in the initial stages by telling you that this is complete nonsense. And of course if you think it's nonsense - you're right - it is! - But you could change your mind!

Ironically, if you did think that this was a load of cobblers and chucked it in the bin - you'd then carry on doing it for the rest of your life. You couldn't NOT do it! - It's how you formed (and are continually re-forming) your world.


## Gratitude

Even if you're broke right now, let your mind dwell on what's good in your life. Count your blessings continually and be thankful for what you have and thankful for what you are receiving.

If you have a roof over your head with mains electricity and running water and enough food in your belly, you're not doing that bad - more so if you are in good health - be thankful!

And if you live in the UK, well you're in the 'Land of Milk and Honey!' Think about:

- Free health care;

- Free housing and other benefits for the needy;

- Stable government and currency;

- Relatively low crime rates;

- Friendly natives;

- Comfortable climate with no extremes etc.

Living in Cyprus for a few years really made me far more appreciative of good old Blighty! - Be thankful!

And let this take over your 'inner chatter' as much as you can. 'I am thankful for the health, wealth and wisdom that I have and am continually receiving' - is a pretty good affirmation to repeat on a regular basis.

Then use your positive declarations as directed but with as much emotion, determination AND BELIEF as possible.

And most importantly - KEEP DOING IT! Everything is governed by 'cause and effect'. Your thoughts the cause - your world the effects! Let me remind you again of the 'Three Wise Monkeys'.

### Binaural Beats

Using Binaural Beats can automatically and effortlessly put you into a relaxed state in order for suggestions/affirmations to have a powerful effect on your subconscious.

They are achieved by playing two very slightly different frequencies (one in each ear via stereo head/ear phones). The brain then creates the 'imaginary' binaural beat which can be clearly heard. For example if the frequency of 100Hz is heard in the left ear and 110Hz in the right ear, the 'ghost' binaural beat of 10Hz will result. And 10Hz is way below the normal hearing range.

The closer the two frequencies are together, the slower the beat will be and therefore generally assisting progressively deeper levels of relaxation.

Tibetan 'singing' bowls can create a similar effect acoustically if used creatively.

Throughout the day (and night) your brainwaves naturally vibrate at varying frequencies ranging from 1.5Hz - 40Hz in the following scale:

| Beta | 15Hz | - | 40Hz | Normal Waking Consciousness / High Awareness |
|-------|-------|---|-------|-----------------------------------------------|
| Alpha | 8Hz | - | 14Hz | Light to Deep Relaxation |
| Theta | 4Hz | - | 8Hz | Deep Relaxation (Meditation) |
| Delta | 0.1Hz | - | 4Hz | Deep Sleep - Coma (total unconsciousness) |

If your brainwaves drop to zero - you're dead! But don't worry as there is in fact no Binaural Beat which could cause this, as if the two frequencies were the same there would be no beat!

When listening to Binaural Beats, your brainwaves will gradual 'attune' to the frequency which causes the temporary alterations in consciousness.

In the 'Alpha' state the mind is relatively open to outside suggestion and consequently this level is ideal for impressing the subconscious with suggestions or affirmations (hypnosis or autosuggestion).

It is generally best to begin the recordings in 'Beta' (normal waking consciousness), gradually step down to the required level and then gradually back to 'Beta' at the end of the session, which is how all of my recordings are produced.

Should you become disturbed while in the 'Alpha', 'Theta' or even 'Delta' states, you may feel a bit 'groggy' (like you've just woken up), and may need a few minutes to re-adjust, but this is nothing that is going to cause you any problems.

The more you use Binaural Beats the easier you will fall into the 'lower' states and consequently the more benefit you will receive.

Please don't think that there is anything unnatural about these states. In certain situations you could be in the Alpha and even Theta states when fully conscious for instance when relaxed and walking through woods etc.

See: http://www.monroeinstitute.org for the most up-to-date work/information and also my site at http://www.deep-relaxation.co.uk.

## Are Binaural Beats/Isochronic Tones safe?

For most individuals binaural/monaural beats and isochronic tones are perfectly safe as they are non addictive and non abusive. However they may not be suitable for a small percentage of the population as indicated here:

- Epilepsy or other seizure sufferers. Due to the effect that the repeating sound pulses may have on the brainwaves, similar to strobe lighting, they could possibly induce a seizure and should therefore be avoided.

- Due to the fact that their brains are still developing, they are not recommended for use by children except under strict medical supervision.

- Anyone who uses a pacemaker or is taking medication (legal or otherwise), should only use brainwave entrainment recordings with medical advice.

If you don't fall into one of the above categories, there's no reason why they can't be used safely and effectively, but of course if you have any negative effects, simply stop using them. If you are in any doubt seek professional medical advice.

**Due to the feelings of relaxation they will induce they should obviously never be used when driving, cycling, cooking, operating machinery or when engaged in any other activity that may put you in danger.**

# Your Free Bonus Downloads

Ok now I'll give you some more information about your free bonus items. Firstly let emphasise that the unique recordings are top quality in every respect, produced using highly sophisticated and specialized recording equipment and also includes a professional voice over (not me).

Your Free downloads include:

- Alpha mp3 with Binaural Beats 30 min recording;

- Alpha mp3 with Isochronic Tones 30 min recording;

- Creativity mp3 (3 x 30 min recordings);

- Prosperity mp3 (2 x 30 min recordings);

- The download links for 5 inspirational books which I mentioned earlier. *I make no claim for these as they are in the public domain, but having the links to hand is very much to your advantage.*

The link for all of these is http://martinwoodward.net/bonus.html but please read the following information about them below.

If you have any trouble with the downloads, please contact me via the contacts page of my website and I'll sort out any problems for you.

**Alpha**

There are two Alpha downloads, both are 30 minutes in length. One uses Binaural Beats and requires stereo head/ear phones, the other uses Isochronic Tones which produces a similar effect but does not require headphones. Both achieve the same results, but you may have a preference which is why I am giving you both.

As mentioned previously these don't have any voice over, just sounds/frequencies which will automatically guide you to the correct level of relaxation for your self-suggestions to be accepted by your subconscious.

These can be used at any time of the day in a solitary relaxed environment enabling you to focus on your affirmations.

Each recording begins and ends in Beta (normal waking consciousness).

All the tracks have Natural sounds and Ambient music etc., but there are periods within in each track where the entrainment beats are unaccompanied and therefore can be heard clearly.

After the initial drop from Beta, the frequencies on these recordings vary between 13hz and 7.5Hz Including:

- 10Hz - Enhanced release of serotonin;

- 9.5Hz - Centre of Alpha;

- 7.83Hz - Earth/Shumann resonance;

- 7.5Hz - Creativity for Music/Art etc.

**Creativity**

This download consists of three 30 minute tracks which can be used to bring out the genius within you. These recordings will take you to a deeper level than the Alpha recordings and it makes no difference whether you consciously listen or not - just lie back and go with the flow! Stereo headphones or earphones are essential for the Binaural Beats to be effective.

Contents are as follows:

**Track 1 - Visualisation - 30 minutes**

- Hypnotic suggestions/awakening, at the beginning and end of recording;

- Natural sounds/Ambient music;

- Binaural Beats, starting in Beta, descending progressively to Theta, then back to Beta at the end.

**Track 2 - Problem Solver - 30 minutes**

- Hypnotic/verbal suggestions for most of the recording;

- Natural sounds/Ambient music/Bells;

- Binaural Beats, starting in Beta, descending progressively to Theta, then back to Beta at the end.

### Track 3 - Innovative Thoughts - 30 minutes

- Hypnotic/verbal suggestions throughout the recording;

- Natural sounds/Ambient music/Bells;

- Binaural Beats, starting in Beta, descending progressively to Theta, then back to Beta at the end.

## Prosperity

This download consists of two 30 minute tracks which can be used to help prepare your mind to accept the prosperity that you deserve. These follow a similar theme to the Creativity recordings and require no effort on your part.

Contents are as follows:

### Track 1 - Abundance - 30 minutes

- Verbal suggestions for most of the recording;

- Natural sounds/Ambient music/Bells;

- No Binaural Beats are on this track.

### Track 2 - Path to Success - 30 minutes

- Hypnotic induction/suggestions/awakening, throughout recording;

- Natural sounds/Ambient music;

- Binaural Beats, starting in Beta, descending progressively to Alpha, briefly into Theta, then back to Beta at the end.

When using any of these recordings, make sure that you adhere to the suitability and safety instructions given previously.

In all cases if you wish to hear the suggestions consciously (perhaps to choose which recording is most suitable to you), you could fast forward to the middle sections and listen without headphones thereby disabling the Binaural Beats.

## Other Books

Links for the following books in the public domain are also included:

- Think and Grow Rich - Napoleon Hill
- The Science of Getting Rich - Wallace Wattles
- The Magic of Believing - Claude M Bristol
- The Secret - Rhonda Byrne
- The Richest Man in Babylon

I urge you to read The Science of Getting Rich first, several times. Don't worry there's only about 60 odd pages, but each time you read it, something new 'clicks'.

## Thanks for Reading this

Thanks for reading this and putting your trust in me enough to buy this book. It's been my sincere desire to provide you with honest quality information and good value for money. I hope that I've succeeded and that you are happy enough to give me some positive feedback from wherever you bought it.

Any problems, I can be contacted via the contacts pages of any of my websites.

My sincerest thanks and best wishes.

Martin

*'Mastering others is strength. Mastering yourself is true power'*

*Lao Tzu.*

**Other Books / Guides by Martin Woodward**

Your Own Home Run Sign Business for Less than £500

Driving Instructor Training - Exposed!

Use Your Mind to Learn to Drive

Clutch Control and Gears Explained!

The New Drivers Handbook

Magnetic Business Cards for Profit

Buy to Let on a Budget

An Introduction to Traded Options

Learn How to Play Electronic Keyboard or Piano in a Week! ♫

Keyboard Improvisation One Note at a Time ♫

Buying Property and Living in Cyprus


See: http://www.martinwoodward.net for details of the above


-----ooooo0000ooooo-----


See: http://www.deep-relaxation.co.uk for details of items below


Binaural Beat Maker Plus

The Golden Sphere

Relaxation CD's & Recordings ♫